Islam Under Siege

Titles in this series

Islam Under Siege

Living Dangerously in a Post-Honor World

AKBAR S. AHMED

polity

First published in 2003 by Polity Press in association with Blackwell Publishing Ltd

Reprinted 2003 (twice), 2004

Editorial and production office:
Polity Press
65 Bridge Street
Cambridge CB2 1UR, UK

Marketing:
Blackwell Publishing Ltd
108 Cowley Road
Oxford OX4 1JF, UK

Distributed in the USA by
Blackwell Publishing Inc.
350 Main Street
Malden, MA 02148, USA

A catalogue record for this book is available from the British Library.

Library of Congress Cataloging-in-Publication Data
Ahmed, Akbar S.
Islam under siege : living dangerously in a post-honor world / Akbar Ahmed.
    p. cm. — (Themes for the 21st century)
Includes bibliographical references and index.
ISBN 0-7456-2209-7 (hb) — ISBN 0-7456-2210-0 (pbk.)
1. Islam—20th century. 2. Islam and world politics. 3.
Globalization—Religious aspects—Islam. I. Title. II. Series.
BP161.3 .A35 2003
297'.09'0511—dc21
    2002154595

Typeset in 10.5 on 12 Plantin
by SetSystems Ltd, Saffron Walden, Essex
Printed and bound in Great Britain by TJ International, Padstow, Cornwall

For further information on Polity, visit our website: www.polity.co.uk

For Larry

in continuation of our discussion about civilizations;
and in gratitude for his scholarship and friendship

Contents

Acknowledgments

Some of the ideas in this book have been developed from lectures, in particular at the Royal Institute of International Affairs, London, and subsequent articles published in its journal *The World Today*; from the inaugural address of the Ibn Khaldun Chair of Islamic Studies at American University, Washington DC, which was published in *The Middle East Journal* (Washington); and from articles published in *The Chronicle of Higher Education* (Washington), *History Today*, *Ethnic and Racial Studies*, the *Independent*, and the *Guardian* (London). The aforementioned are gratefully acknowledged. A special thanks to Religion News Service, USA.

I am grateful to the following for their comments: Amineh Ahmed, David Godwin, Louis Goodman, Carole O'Leary, Peter Lewis, James Mittelman, Joe Montville, Mustapha Kamal Pasha, Chris Rojek, Todd Sedmak, and Tamara Sonn. I wish to acknowledge Kathleen Cahill of the *Washington Post* for her invaluable assistance in helping to edit the book and making suggestions to clarify the issues it raises. As always my wife, Zeenat, inspired me with her commitment to my work, oversaw the writing of the book and helped me in refining my ideas. The book is dedicated to our friend Professor Lawrence Rosen of Princeton University in acknowledgment of his scholarship and friendship.

Akbar S. Ahmed

Introduction: God's Gamble

"There will be a time when your religion will be like a hot piece of coal in the palm of your hand; you will not be able to hold it." The Prophet of Islam was gazing into the future while he talked to his followers early in the 7th century in Arabia. "Would this mean there would be very few Muslims?" someone asked later. "No," replied the Prophet, "They will be large in numbers, more than ever before, but powerless like the foam on the ocean waves."

After September 11, 2001, the prediction of the Prophet seemed to be coming true. Islam became as hot as a piece of coal for its followers. Yet it had more followers than ever before and they were, for the first time, spread all over the globe. Muslim societies everywhere appeared to be in turmoil and Muslims felt themselves in the dock, accused of belonging to a "terrorist," "fanatic," and "extremist" religion. Islam, it seemed, was under siege.

The "war on terrorism" that President George Bush declared after September 11 threatens to stretch into the century; for many Muslims it appears to be a war against Islam. For a Muslim therefore, on both a global and personal level, this is a time of challenge and despair.

As an anthropologist I will try to make sense of a changing, complicated, and dangerous world. I will attempt to explain *what* is going wrong in the Muslim world; *why* it is going wrong, and *how* we, because my explanation involves Muslims and non-Muslims, are to move ahead if we wish for global stability and even harmony in the future.

I will use the methodology of reflexive anthropology and give examples of a personal nature to illustrate a point. I will also raise questions and suggest possible future exploratory directions. I do not pretend to have the answers. A multiplicity of interpretations is possible. Old concepts are being debated or rejected.

Rupture, change, and attempts at religious reform have been evident in Muslim societies over the last two centuries since the advent of Western colonization. Certain technological and economic developments further exacerbate the divisions and debate within society. The ideological frame within which Muslim normative behavior and thought is to be understood is itself being challenged. Muslim normative behavior cannot be understood without the Quran – for Muslims the word of God – and the life of the Prophet; together the two form the *Shari'a* or the Path.

Muslims everywhere are being forced to reassess and re-examine Islam. Questions are being raised about God and the purpose of creation. There are questions also about the tenets of Islam itself and what its future holds.

God's gamble

In order to understand our world it is necessary to remember that God does not play dice with the universe. Einstein was right. But in creating human beings and giving them free will God did gamble with history. Seeing the state of affairs in the early 21st century – the widespread poverty, the lack of justice and compassion, the willful depletion of the resources of the planet, the senseless and widespread violence – God may well be regretting human creation now. And we have a good idea of what He had in mind. Through inspired messengers and sacred literature God conveyed the idea to man and woman that they were created in His own image. (Contrary to the widely held stereotype of Islam as a misogynist religion, the Quran addresses and includes both men and women.) The Quran describes man as God's "deputy" or "vicegerent" (Surah 2: Verse 30).[1]

God took a gamble by creating human beings. There is a central and cruel tension in the very idea of free will: Man has the capacity to kill and destroy just as easily as to be just and compassionate. This implies a certain confidence on the part of God that human beings would use their learning and instincts to suppress the wild and anarchic impulse of their nature. God wants humans to do good and to avoid evil (Surah 9: Verse 112). He wants justice and balance in human society (Surah 55: Verse 9). What perhaps would disappoint God the most, therefore, are the extreme expressions of violence of which humans are capable, especially now that they have developed their genius to change and control their environment. The marvelous achievements in medicine and communications have not subdued man's rapacious appetite. Human society is not even prepared to accept that it is busily destroying the planet. Arguments about depriving future generations appear to fall on deaf ears.

God's vision of Himself in the Quran is also explicit. So while God sees Himself as omnipotent and omnipresent, He also emphasizes justice and compassion. He describes Himself as the God of the universes – note the use of the plural. For us here on earth God makes it clear that for Him there are no artificial divisions within human society based on tribe or color. Geographically, too, there is neither East nor West for Him (Surah 2: Verse 115). He is everywhere and belongs to everyone. God made people into different tribes and nations speaking different languages and living in different cultures: All these are signs of God's universal compassion and we must learn to appreciate each other (Surah 5: Verse 48, Surah 30: Verse 22, and Surah 49: Verse 13). He even sent messengers like Abraham who are common to several religions – in this case Judaism, Christianity, and Islam. Above all, God declared: "There is no compulsion in religion" (Surah 2: Verse 256).

Everything was from God and the more man was in the image of God the closer he was to fulfilling his destiny and becoming God's "deputy." It is in this context that the idea of merging with God, which finds historic expression in the Sufi dictum *ana al-haqq* or "I am God," can be understood. Although the idea was sacrilegious to the orthodox it was not as far-fetched as it seemed. By God wishing to create divine qualities in man, He was emphasizing the unity and integration of creation itself.[2]

Of all the attributes developed in human beings, perhaps the greatest is the capacity to make moral choices: Humans are the only species that can turn the other cheek in the face of provocation or speak of peace with others. In their expression of compassion, humans reflect the divine spark that connects them to their maker.

If an angel, skeptical about human beings, were to query God about what humans had achieved in their short history on earth, God could point to His greatest gift to them: creative genius. He could point to the devotion and piety of the Abrahamic prophets; the wisdom of Buddha and Confucius; the building of the pyramids and the Taj Mahal; the human predicament and nobility depicted in the literature of the ages – the Vedas, the *Iliad*, and the

Shakespearean plays; the poetry of Rumi and Ghalib; the discovery of nuclear technology and the marvels of modern science and communications; the inventiveness that allowed humans to fly in the sky, live under water, and walk on the moon. Most of these cases of creativity are invested with moral choices.

Similar moral choices have allowed human beings to use the name of God to wreak violence on others who believed in Him in different ways. Indeed, they were neglectful and cruel even to those who came with His message. Moses returned from Mount Sinai where he had gone to receive God's message to discover that his followers had created a golden calf and were worshiping it. Jesus was tortured and crucified. The Prophet of Islam may have escaped assassination attempts but three of his four successors – good and pious men – did not. Later, the four men most influential in shaping Islamic law were flogged and imprisoned. One died in jail.

God's categories of human behavior

In order to become God's deputy, according to Islam, human beings had to follow two categories of behavior and ensure a balance between them. The first related to rituals and prayers and was primarily designed to create a relationship between man and God. It included the five pillars of Islam: the declaration of belief in God; fasting; praying; paying charity (in cash or in kind); and going on the pilgrimage to Mecca once in a lifetime. Although these five pillars required interaction with others they were primarily related to individual action. And they created the conditions to engender the second category of social action.

That second category created, and was embedded in, broader social relations. Of these the most important are *adl* (justice), *ihsan* (compassion, kindness and balance), and *ilm* (knowledge; *ilm* is the second most used word in the Quran after the name of Allah or God). But *adl*, justice, was only possible if it was made available in society by judges and rulers. Similarly *ihsan*, compassion or balance, could only be achieved if others in society believed in it and helped to realize it. The acquisition of *ilm*, knowledge, although an individual act, was nonetheless only possible if society provided libraries, colleges, and colleagues to enhance it. Even if knowledge was acquired it was difficult to share or develop in repressive societies. Implementing knowledge meant changing society. Justice, compassion, and knowledge had enormous implications for the kind of society God desired. They also created the preconditions for ideal leadership. A leader who believed in them was a good leader.

Together, the two categories provided the conditions that created a just society. The first category rested on a vertical axis and its primary understanding was through the filter of theology; the second on a horizontal axis and its primary filter was that of anthropology. Together, they formed the Islamic ideal. To discover the ideal we thus need a polythetic, not monothetic, analysis of contemporary Muslim society.

Religious systems must balance individual piety with public interaction. What is important for all of us looking for ways to live together in spite of the different religions and races to which we belong is not so much whether believing in one God (as in the Abrahamic faiths) is better than believing in many gods (Hinduism), or even in no god (Buddhism), but of creating a balanced, compassionate, and harmonious society with decent, caring people in it.

The failure to create a just and compassionate society leads people to fall back to ideas of tribal honor and revenge. Divisions in society deepen on the basis of blood and custom. Killing and conflict are encouraged. The honor of the group and – if it is attacked – the need to take revenge become more important than worshiping God in peace and engendering compassion in society.

Why is Islam important?

The 21st century will be the century of Islam. The events of September 11 saw to that. The hijackers of the four American planes killed not only thousands of innocent people. Their terrible act also created one of the greatest paradoxes of the 21st century: Islam, which sees itself as a religion of peace, is now associated with murder and mayhem. Consider Islam today: There are about 1.3 billion Muslims living in 55 states (one, for the time being, nuclear; about one-third of the world's Muslims live in non-Muslim countries); about 25 million live in the West (including 7 million in the USA and 2 million in the UK); and Muslim nations are indispensable for American foreign policy (of the nine "pivotal" states on which the United States bases its foreign policy, five are Muslim – see Chase et al. 1996). The Muslim world population is one of the fastest growing. And Islam is the one world religion which appears to be on a collision course with the other world religions.

We know that for the first time in history, due to a unique geopolitical conjunction of factors, Islam is in confrontation with all of the major world religions: Judaism in the Middle East, Christianity in the Balkans, Chechnya, Nigeria, Sudan, and sporadically in the Philippines and Indonesia; Hinduism in South Asia, and, after the Taliban blew up the statues in Bamiyan, Buddhism. The Chinese, whose culture represents an amalgam of the philosophy of Confucius, Tao, and Communist ideology, are also on a collision course with Islam in China's western province.

It is this historic conjunction that both singles out Islam and creates the global argument that the 21st century will be a time of war between Islam and the other world civilizations. Of course, this neat concept is challenged because so many Muslim countries are clearly allied to non-Muslim ones. Besides, so many Muslims now live in non-Muslim nations. But it is true to say that the major world civilizations are experiencing problems in accommodating or even understanding Islam, both within their borders and outside them.

Whatever the economic, political, and sometimes demographic causes of social transformations on this scale, simplistic ideas often capture the imagination and become the filter through which ordinary people understand them. One such idea has now firmly caught the imagination of people across the world – that there is an ongoing clash between Islam and Western civilization. The argument has been stoked by Harvard professors and by European prime ministers, but it has been around for a thousand years. Whether one adheres to the notion of the clash of civilizations, or whether one chooses dialogue, understanding Islam will be key.

Islamophobia – or a generalized hatred or contempt of Islam and its civilization – appears to be widespread and growing. This is the reality on the ground – however grand and noble even the best-written constitutions and charters. The result is pressure on the Muslim family and on social, political, and even moral life. The consequence is anger, confusion, and frustration; acts of violence result. *Fitna* and *shar*, chaos and conflict, become common. God's vision of a just and compassionate human society remains unfulfilled. Understanding Islam thus becomes important.

The consequences of what happens within Muslim society will be felt by societies everywhere. No one is immune from the debates that now rage around Islam. The issues outlined in this book will concern scholars, policy-makers and ordinary citizens.

Misunderstanding Islam

Yet there is so much misunderstanding of Islam. The debate on Islam that is in full cry in the West since September 11 is too often little more than a parading of deep-rooted prejudices. For example, the critics of Islam ask: "If there is such an emphasis on compassion and tolerance in Islam, why is it associated with violence and intolerance toward non-Muslims[3] and the poor treatment of women?"[4]

The answer is that both Muslims and non-Muslims use the Quran selectively. The Quranic verses revealed earlier, for example, Surah 2: Verses 190–4, emphasize peace and reconciliation in comparison to the latter ones like Surah 9: Verse 5. Some activists have argued that this means an abrogation of the earlier verses and therefore advocate aggressive militancy. In fact the verses have to be understood in the social and political context in which they were formed. They must be read both for the particular situation in which they were revealed and the general principle they embody.

Take the first criticism of Islam: that it encourages violence. The actions of the nineteen hijackers had little to do with Islamic theology. Killing a single innocent person is like killing all of humanity, warns the Quran (Surah 5: Verse 32). The Quran clearly preaches tolerance and understanding. Indeed, there is an anthropologically illuminating verse which points to the diversity of races: "O Human Beings! Behold, We have created you all out of a male and a female and have made you into nations and tribes so that you might come to know one another . . . The noblest of you, in the sight of God, is the best in conduct" (Surah 49: Verse 13).

The idea of a common humanity is central to the Muslim perception of self. By knowing God as *Rahman* and *Rahim*, Beneficent and Merciful – the two most frequently repeated of God's 99 names, those that God Himself has chosen in the Quran by using them to introduce the chapters – Muslims know they must embrace even those who may not belong to their community, religion, or nation. God tells us in the Quran to appreciate the variety He has created in human society: "And of His signs is the creation of the heavens and the earth, and the difference of your languages and colors. Lo! Herein indeed are portents for men of knowledge" (Surah 30: Verse 22).

Verses about fighting Jews and Christians – or Muslims who are considered "hypocrites" – must be understood relative to a specific situation and time frame. What is important for Muslims is to stand up for their rights whoever the aggressor: "Fight against those who fight against you, but begin not hostilities," the Quran tells Muslims (Surah 2: Verse 190). Men like bin Laden cite this verse and the next to justify their violence against Jews and Christians in general and in particular the United States, which represents the two religions for them. They give the impression that God wants Muslims to be in perpetual conflict with Jews and Christians. They are wrong. Not only are these verses taken out of context, as they relate to a specific situation at a certain time in the history of early Islam, but the verses that follow immediately after clearly convey God's overarching command: "Make peace with them if they want peace; God is Forgiving, Merciful" (Surah 2: Verses 192–3).

Misguided Muslims and non-Muslims, especially the instant experts in the media, are both guilty of this kind of selective use of the holy text to support their arguments. In this case the Muslims would argue that violence against Jews and Christians is allowed; the non-Muslims would point to this line and say it confirms the hatred of Muslims against others. They imply that the idea of fighting against Islam is therefore justified.

The discussion around the number of women a Muslim man may marry suffers from a similar fate (see below chapter 4, section ii, "Veiled Truth: Women in Islam"). Misguided Muslims cite Surah 4: Verse 3 – "Marry as many women as you wish, two or three or four" – to justify having four wives; misguided non-Muslims, to point to Islam's licentious nature. Both ignore the next line in the same verse, which insists that each wife be treated equally and with "justice" and, as this is not possible, then one wife is the best arrangement.

"Why do they hate us?"

For many – and not only Muslims – there is another side to the age we live in, one that feeds anger. The images of people being killed in Palestine or Kashmir or Chechnya create helplessness and outrage. Directly or indirectly many people blame the United States. To them, the superpower is morally bankrupt and unwilling to halt the suffering in the world or stop its own obsessive consumerism. The United States was hated long before bin Laden forced George Bush to ask the question, "Why do they hate us?"

At the core of the recent animosity toward Islam were the young Muslims prepared to commit suicide for their beliefs. "Why?" the West asked. The answers flooded the media: "They hate us"; "They envy our lifestyle"; "They hate our democracy." In a country where psychiatrists hold sway in interpreting behavior, where they are consulted like high priests, where one of the most popular television shows, *Frasier*, features two brothers who are psychiatrists, it was natural that the hijackers' actions would be cast in psychiatric terms: "envy," "hatred," "jealousy."

Other commentators gave other explanations. The Reverend Jerry Falwell thundered about God's wrath and blamed homosexuality, abortion, and loose morals in American society. Samuel Huntington was frequently cited and must have smirked with satisfaction as the attacks seemed to confirm what he had said all along about the clash of civilizations between Muslims and the West (1993, 1996). Salman Rushdie gloated that he had been right all along about Islam: "Yes, this is about Islam" (*New York Times*, November 2, 2001). Francis Fukuyama was on the defensive as his theories of the triumph of capitalism and the end of history (1998)[5] lay in the rubble of New York and the Pentagon. History had not ended on September 11; it had been jump-started in new and dangerous directions.[6]

For people in developing societies the "war on terrorism" is in fact a violent expression of the rapacious, insatiable, and minatory engine of American imperialism:

> The Task That Never Ends is America's perfect war, the perfect vehicle for the endless expansion of American imperialism. In Urdu, the word for profit is *fayda*. Al-qaida means the word, the word of God, the law. So, in India, some of us call the War Against Terror, Al-qaida vs Al-fayda – the Word vs The Profit (no pun intended). For the moment it looks as though Al-fayda will carry the day. But then you never know . . . ("Not Again" by Arundhati Roy in the *Guardian*, September 27, 2002)

The answers in the media were not only incomplete; they were pushing the debate in the wrong directions.

Hate and prejudice substituted for thought and analysis. The social sciences could have provided answers. Yet in all the discussion of suicide attacks, I did not once hear the name of Emile Durkheim, whose seminal work on suicide informs scholarly discussions (*Suicide: A Study in Sociology*, 1966 edition; also see Giddens 1978; for a contemporary overview of Durkheim see Poggi 2000).

Durkheim underlined that traditional explanations of suicide, such as mental disturbance, race, or climate, did not fully explain the act. He argued that suicide was a consequence of a disturbed social order. Moral codes were disrupted in times of change and affected rich and poor, he wrote. The strain led to suicide and abnormal behavior, which he identified as "anomie" (*The Division of Labour in Society*, 1964 edition). Durkheim was echoing Abd al-Rahman bin Muhammad Ibn Khaldun's *asabiyya*; the word derives from the Arabic root *assab* which means "to bind" (Dhaouadi 1997: 12). The nearest definitions of *asabiyya* are "group loyalty," "social cohesion," or "social solidarity" (which I discuss below). These two thinkers provide us with a useful central thesis: We need to look for answers in the changing social order; in the sense of social breakdown; the feeling of the loss of honor and dignity. This is what I will do.

Outline of the argument

September 11, 2001, threw up a range of questions about Islam. Does the Quran preach violence? Do Muslims hate Jews and Christians? Are we at the start of a final crusade between Islam and the West? Why is the message of peace and compassion of the world's religions lost in the din of anger and hatred? How can local cultures retain their sense of identity and dignity in the face of the onslaught of global developments? Is the perception of the loss of honor a consequence of the disintegration of group loyalty or social cohesion in society? Can we identify cause and effect? Is group loyalty, tempered by humanistic compassion, the way forward?

Given the high degree of uncertainty surrounding these questions it is not surprising that many of the answers in recent years have been superficial or shoddy. Even the experts can get it wrong. While anthropology can assist us in answering these questions we will also need to rely on other disciplines. But this book is not about anthropology. Nor is it about bin Laden. It is about the world that has created bin Laden and his Al-Qaeda network and the world he has helped to create. It is about bin Laden's religion, Islam, which, by his actions, has been put on a collision course with other world religions. This book, then, is an exercise in mapping the global landscape and pointing out the routes – and dangers – that lie ahead.

I am exploring alternative concepts to postmodernism,[7] postemotionalism,[8] and posthuman[9] to explain our world. I suggest we are entering a "post-honor" world (see chapter 2, section ii, "A Post-Honor World?").[10] I am suggesting we explore the notion of honor and its use in our time as a tool with which to look at our world. We cannot do so without reference to society and its ideas of *asabiyya*, group loyalty, cohesion, or solidarity. If the definition of honor is changed then we need to examine society to understand why this has happened. I argue that it is a consequence of a new variety of *asabiyya* which is based in an exaggerated and even obsessive loyalty to the group and which is usually expressed through hostility and often violence toward the other. I call this hyper-*asabiyya*. I am pointing to cause and effect here. However, mine is merely an exploratory effort, suggesting possible future research.

I will argue that the dangerously ambiguous notion of

honor – and the even more dangerous idea of the loss of honor – propels men to violence. Simply put, global developments have robbed many people of honor. Rapid global changes are shaking the structures of traditional societies. Groups are forced to dislocate or live with or by other groups. In the process of dislocation they have little patience with the problems of others. They develop intolerance and express it through anger. No society is immune. Even those societies that economists call "developed" fall back to notions of honor and revenge in times of crisis.

By dishonoring others, such people think they are maintaining honor. They are, therefore, challenging traditional notions of honor, which rested in doing good deeds and pursuing noble causes. In times past, chivalry acknowledged courage, compassion, and generosity even if found in the enemy. Women and the weak were given special treatment by honorable men. The pursuit of honor was thus a humanistic goal. Cruelty and tyranny were usually condemned as deviations from the ideal of honor. In contrast many in our time consider it honorable to indulge in acts of violence. What would once have been seen as the deviant appears to be accepted as the norm. Exaggerated tribal and religious loyalties – hyper-*asabiyya* – disguise acts of violence against the other. But neither tribal custom nor religious ideology requires the senseless violence we witness in our time. The widespread use of honor in this perverted manner suggests we may indeed be living in a world with little honor or no honor or a post-honor world. Hyper-*asabiyya* is cause and symptom of the post-honor world in which we live.

Let me explain how our world works. Take bin Laden, one of the best-known warriors of the post-honor world – and alas there are many like him and not only in Muslim society as we will see below. Bin Laden identifies excessively with his group as the traditional markers of identity – family, nation, religion – appear under threat. He blames others for their plight – in his case Jews and Christians or Americans, that is citizens of the United States. (In his confused state he fuses religious and national identity.) To correct the situation and reclaim honor he plans to inflict violence on Americans. He does not care if innocent people, including women and children, are killed. He does not even care if Muslims are killed – as indeed they were in the attacks on New York in September 2001.

Bin Laden's behavior provides us with clues of why men interpret honor to mean violence and how they implement their vision to regain it. Hyper-*asabiyya* encourages a mutated, twisted, and violent interpretation of honor and creates conditions for post-honor society.

Honor and revenge; this is the male interpretation of social action. It is no coincidence that the *dramatis personae* on the world stage after September 11 are mainly male – George Bush, Richard Cheney, Colin Powell, and Donald Rumsfeld in the United States; Tony Blair in the UK; Vladimir Putin in Russia; Ariel Sharon, Yasser Arafat, Hosni Mubarak, Saddam Hussein, and the two Abdullahs (the Hashemite King of Jordan and the Saudi Crown Prince) in the Middle East; Osama bin Laden, Muhammad Umar, the Taliban, and Hamid Karzai in Afghanistan; and Pervez Musharraf in Pakistan. Nearly all the Americans recognized in the American media as the "heroes" of September 11 – the Mayor of New York, the fire-fighters, and the police officers who died on duty – were male.

To reverse the movement that has brought us into a post-honor world we need to rediscover the dialogue with and understanding of cultures other than our own. We need to emphasize a morality that emphasizes justice and compassion for all.

The problem is that so many traditional definitions – and not only those of honor – are under challenge. We can no longer accept the notion of a world divided between opposing halves – Islam versus the West – as did Muslim activists for most of the 20th century (for example, Maulana Syed Abul Ala Maududi in South Asia and Sayyid Qutb in the Middle East). The emergence of more than 25 million Muslims living in the West, the clashes between Hindus and Muslims in India, and Muslims and other Chinese in China, and the conflict within Muslim society based on ethnicity (the Northern Alliance versus the Taliban in Afghanistan, for example) suggest that such simplistic division is no longer valid.

I will therefore use the terms "Islam" and "the West" as shorthand, but with the caveat that reducing these two highly complex and internally diverse civilizations to such simplistic terms may create more problems than it solves. We will therefore continue to color in gray, however great the compulsion to use black and white.

Besides, the traditional Muslim division of the world has collapsed: What Muslims once saw as the distinction between *dar al-harb* (the house of war), land of anarchy and disbelief, and *dar al-Islam* (the house of peace or Islam) in which they could practice their faith and flourish, is no longer valid.[11] In the last decades of the 20th century the division became largely irrelevant. Muslims could freely practice their faith and flourish in the United States and elsewhere; meanwhile they were persecuted in Iraq. After September 2001, the distinction disappeared altogether. Muslims everywhere felt under siege. Nowhere was safe. No society was immune to the forces of chaos and anarchy. Violence was routine. The entire world had become *dar al-harb*.

For help in understanding the struggle taking place within the Muslim world, I shall turn to the work of one of the earliest and most penetrating Muslim social scientists, Ibn Khaldun (1332–1406). Ibn Khaldun's theory of *asabiyya* appears to glorify religious or tribal group loyalty in contradiction to Islam which emphasizes the universal and the compassionate. There is thus an inherent problem for a Muslim group in adopting a parochial position. But what group social cohesion does is to provide stability and continuity in normal times. For minorities too it ensures protection and justice. I will point out how Muslim *asabiyya* has generally collapsed and how society itself, consequently, has moved away from not only traditional patterns of behavior but also the central features of Islam itself. This has far-reaching implications. I will give examples of the collapse of Islamic leadership and scholarship. I will discuss how Muslims are responding to the crisis, in part by considering the cultural notions of honor and dignity. There is clearly a cultural dimension to our understanding of political and religious issues.

"Fundamentalist," "terrorist," and "extremist" – these words have become meaningless for us today. Can we apply terms such as "fundamentalist" without creating more problems than we resolve? Can we use terms created for one religion – in this case Christianity – and apply them to another religion – Islam? Isn't every Muslim a "fundamentalist" as he or she believes in the "fundamentals" of the Quran? Do not even liberal Muslims believe in the essential divinity of the Quran? But is every Muslim a "fanatic" or "terrorist" or "extremist"? The answer is clearly no. So terms like "fundamentalist" tell us little and those like "terrorist" and "extremist" tell us even less. Their usage only adds to the confusion. I will explore the use of other terms and definitions.

"Exclusivist" and "inclusivist" have the merits of simplicity and clarity. They incorporate notions such as fundamentalist, terrorist, and extremist. Exclusivists create boundaries and believe in hierarchies; inclusivists are those who are prepared to accommodate, to interact with others, and even listen to them and be influenced by them. Inclusivists are those who believe that human civilization is essentially one, however much we are separated by religion, culture, or language. These frames of reference exist in every human society. Many adherents of mainstream religions, for example, are dogmatists who simply do not accept even those who belong to a different sect of the same religion. I believe the real battle in the 21st century will be between the inclusivists and the exclusivists. I am defining these two categories broadly, while aware of the many variations, differences, and changing positions within them.

We need to tease out the nuances. Global transformations and dislocations threaten traditional societies and force them to regroup around rigid boundaries. While the exclusivists provide social cohesion and group loyalty that provide continuity and stability in society, a too rigid application of exclusivity results in violence against the other. Exclusivism to a point is required but needs to be tempered with compassion and justice. Otherwise exclusivism will lead to confrontation and conflict.

One of the problems the inclusivists face is the preference the media give to the exclusivists. Messages of conflict and confrontation are considered more newsworthy than what is seen as the bland and vapid talk of dialogue. More importantly, within society the sense of anger in the Muslim community discourages support for the inclusivists. There are too many examples of injustice in the Muslim world for the inclusivists to be able to talk of dialogue with conviction. Simple solutions suggesting immediate action are more popular than laborious and uncertain bouts of conversation. Besides, the demography of the Muslim world clearly indicates that a very high percentage of the population is young; this, correlated with the low literacy rates, means that emotional and angry solutions find a greater audience and wider appeal.

The hostile global environment against Islam encourages the exclusivists. Scholars like Richard Falk, at Princeton University, have argued that in the age of globalization there is a deliberate attempt to "exclude" Muslims from the community of world civilizations, to make them pariahs, non-persons (see the chapter "The Geo-Politics of Exclusion: The Case of Islam" in Falk 2000).

Through two extended case studies in the pages that follow I shall examine Muslim societies and how and where they are failing in God's commands. Employing the method of reflexive anthropology I will offer a personal account of an attempt to create understanding through several projects, one of which has come to be known as the Jinnah Quartet. At the risk of exposing events from my life, the small achievements and the failures, over the last few years, I will discuss the problems I faced in developing the Quartet. My aim will not be to blow my own trumpet but to point out the problems that can arise in Muslim society when one attempts a certain direction within and for it. The exercise will also allow us to look inside the working and thinking of Muslim society.

In the second case I shall focus on the Taliban, which illuminated the paradox that pious Muslims can indeed fail to create a truly Islamic society by too exclusivist an approach. They obey one set of commands – the five pillars – and ignore the second; there was little justice or compassion or knowledge in the Taliban's treatment of women and minorities. By emphasizing the first category and minimizing the second, they create societal imbalance. The failure to follow the tenets of the second category, as we shall see, is notable, and the implications of that failure are great.

I will also consider globalization, noting how compli-cated and volatile life will be in this century even with some understanding of the processes of globalization (see the next two chapters for a discussion of globalization). My arguments may suggest to some that a clash between Islam and the West is inevitable and that, indeed, I may be endorsing the idea of a clash of civilizations. On the contrary, I wish to point out that in the heat and noise of the discussion about such a clash there is emerging a quiet but powerful current for an alternative: the dialogue of civilizations.

My concluding chapter suggests the need for dialogue. That may be unrealistic in the face of the global hostility to Islam and the practical difficulties in Muslim societies at a time when Muslim leadership appears bankrupt of vision and indifferent to the condition of its societies. But the idea of dialogue – dialogue *between* civilizations and *within* civilizations – promises hope. By repeating the word "dialogue" perhaps it will be transformed from a cliché to a meaningful bridge of understanding between groups. People of good will and good faith can generate dialogue, which is sane, balanced, and urgently required, given the state of the post-honor world (see chapters 5 and 7). If dialogue is to be productive then the exclusivists, in whichever cultural or political tradition they operate, need to curb their "I am right and everyone else is wrong" tendency.

We need, however, to move beyond the empty words "dialogue" and "understanding." We should consider the universal message of the Sufis of South Asia who advocate *sulh-i-kul* or "peace with all." Perhaps they had the answer when they first came to India a thousand years ago. Their *sulh-i-kul* reflected the core ideas of a compassionate divinity – after all, as we have noted, the two greatest names of God are Beneficent and Merciful. Only through

1

Islam Under Siege

i The Return of Anthropology and the Final Crusade

Anthropology has much for which to thank bin Laden. After decades of criticism, anthropology was on the ropes not long ago. Its founding fathers and mothers were discredited: Bronislaw Malinowski for lusting after young natives and Margaret Mead for cooking up ethnographic accounts. Its own practitioners despaired and predicted "The End of Anthropology" (title of Worsley 1966; see also Banaji 1970). When the field appeared at its weakest, the powerful new voice of Edward Said emerged to denounce it as tainted by the dreaded word "Orientalism" (title of Said 1978). Perhaps the unkindest cut was that anthropology was not even seen as a bulldog in the service of the Western imperialists but rather as a mere puppy. Students of anthropology wandered aimlessly – sometimes into post-modernist literary conceit and sometimes into autobiographical excess. Like John Keats's knight in "La Belle Dame Sans Merci," anthropology appeared to be "ailing." It appeared "alone and palely loitering."

September 11 changed all that. The main interests of anthropology – ideas of ethnicity, group loyalty, honor, revenge, suicide, tribal code, the conflict between what anthropologists call the Great Tradition of world religions and their local practice or the Little Tradition – were being discussed everywhere. Perhaps people were not even aware that they were discussing these issues as they were identified with traditional, even "primitive" societies, and therefore discredited; now they were front-page news. What was clear was the sense of hyper-*asabiyya* – and the accompanying paranoia and uncertainty.

Ironically, most religions and communities across the globe felt they were under siege. American television broadcast its news and discussions under the title "America under Siege"; Israelis felt the Arabs had besieged them; and Indians complained of being hemmed in by aggressive Muslim neighbors. The United States, Israel, and India appeared paralyzed in the face of Muslim suicide bombers. They had no answer to the violence except more violence.

With each killing the siege mentality spread. State strategy appeared to be to use more brute power and inflict more pain on the opposite side. Where vision and compassion were required, the state was seen to kill and maim people and destroy property. Its representatives did not even spare the mosque, the house of God.

The United States, Israel, and India were compromising hard-won ideas of a modern, thriving democracy. There were cases of illegal detention, suspension of civil liberties, and unauthorized surveillance. The victim was invariably a Muslim.

Muslims, whether living as a majority, or a minority, felt especially vulnerable after September 11. The fact that all 19 of the hijackers were Muslim appeared to condemn by association every Muslim on the planet. Any expression of Muslim identity risked the fear of being suspected as "terrorist" activity. Muslims felt that their religion Islam was under siege.

The road to the Crusades

In the last years of the 20th century a general if amorphous perception had begun to form in the West that with the fall of Communism the new global enemy would be Islam. The idea crystallized on September 11. Bush's declaration of a "crusade" against the "Islamic terrorists" followed. In the wake of the negative media response abroad to the word "crusade" Bush swiftly dropped it. However the Freudian slip had hinted to some that the war would indeed be a crusade against Islam. Other world leaders were less sensitive than Bush about the use of the word "crusade." Silvio Berlusconi, the Italian prime minister, declared publicly that Islam was the main enemy of Western civilization.

But who represented Islam? Was it bin Laden and Al-Qaeda or a specific nation or nations or the entire Muslim world? If the definition of the enemy was vague, the length of the war was even vaguer; nor were the boundaries of the theater of operations any clearer. The full might of the United States would be used against the "terrorists" wherever they were to be found and the war would be indefinitely waged until the enemy was destroyed. Private media and official institutions came together in a formidable spirit of determined unity. Clearly this was going to be more than a military campaign managed by the Pentagon to fight a small group hiding in the caves of Afghanistan.

By thinking and acting in crusader mode Bush was rejecting ideas of multi-religious multiculturalism. He was rejecting postmodernist pluralism and reviving what writers and artists called the Grand or Meta Narrative, which underlines domination by a monolithic idea or culture. In pursuing his war on terrorism Bush, with his "You are with us or against us" approach, also was rolling back the postmodern age to a time of certitude, defined borders, and monolithic ideas. He had turned the clock back a thousand years. Once again the West was launching armies against Muslim lands and people; once again the dividing line was to be religion; once again ideas of honor, revenge, dignity, culture, and community became important.

Bush's adversary bin Laden was rejecting the West, which he saw as corrupting. He talked of the loss of honor among Muslim leaders, of the plight of the Palestinians and the Iraqis, and of the loss of dignity of his own people, the Saudis, due to the presence of American troops. To him the United States was evil and had to be battled. (For the story of another Muslim, Ajab Khan, who challenged – and temporarily shook – a Western superpower see chapter 2, section ii).

The protagonists recognized early in the struggle that this crusade was about changing minds, not conquering territory. But with wedding party guests being killed in Afghanistan by American bombing, it was hard to expect the good will earned in removing the Taliban to last. In the end, to ordinary Afghans, being killed by Bush's bombs or those of bin Laden made little difference.[1]

Matters were made worse because of the mutual lack of understanding. Americans associated empty caves in the Afghan mountains, the firing of weapons into the sky, and the storage of ammunition and weapons with terrorist activity. For the people of the region, however, for generations caves had meant nomadic tribes moving to cooler climes in summer; firing into the sky a mark of celebration at birth and marriage; and the storage of weapons an insurance against tribal rivalries.

So far, two crusades have pitted the West against Islam. The first began in the 11th century and, after several waves of European warriors were exhausted, ended in the 13th. The second, which took the form of straightforward

European colonization, occupied the 19th and first half of the 20th century. Both crusades began with triumph for the West and the capture of Muslim lands, but both ultimately failed.

Both have been seen as a clash of military forces but they were also a competition of cultural and intellectual ideas. The West was at a distinct disadvantage one thousand years ago as Muslim civilization was already established as the pre-eminent cultural and political force. It was the time of rulers like Saladin, who on recapturing Jerusalem from the Crusaders could show magnanimity in spite of vowing to avenge their bloody massacres. It was the age of the towering scholars and mystics of Islam – Muhyiddin Ibn Arabi,[2] Abdullah Ibn Sina, Abu Raihan Al-Beruni, Abu Hamid Al-Ghazzali, and Jalal al-Din al-Rumi, to name a few.[3] Their prose and poetry reflect inspiration from the Torah, the Bible, and the Quran; from Moses, Jesus, and Muhammad (peace be upon them). When Rumi died, a Christian is on record as being asked why he wept so bitterly, and his answer was: "We esteem him as the Moses, the David, the Jesus of the age. We are all his followers and his disciples" (Shah 1990: 149). Not surprisingly the early makers of European consciousness – Aquinas, Dante, and Cervantes – were influenced by what was seen as the irresistible global culture influenced by Islam.

As late as the 17th century, Muslim rulers were advocating tolerance. Akbar the Great in India ordered his governors to spend their spare time reading Al-Ghazzali and Rumi. On the main entrance to his grand city Fatehpur Sikri, soon to be deserted for lack of water, Akbar inscribed the following lines: "Jesus, on whom be peace, has said: This world is a bridge. Pass over it. But build not your dwelling there" (Jeremias 1964: 112; his section titled "The World is a Bridge" on p. 111 discusses the origins of this saying and its attribution to both Jesus and the Prophet of Islam).

Akbar's grandson Dara Shikoh carried on the tradition of tolerance by wearing a ring inscribed with "Prabhu," the Sanskritic name for God, keeping the company of yogis, and patronizing translations of the *Upanishads* and *Bhagawad Gita* into Persian. Dara Shikoh was not renouncing Islam, and his ideal remained the Prophet of Islam. But his tolerance cost him his life. The Muslim world was already changing.

The situation between Islam and the West was reversed two centuries later when Europeans slowly but inexorably colonized Muslim lands in the imperialist crusade. This time Europeans could dismiss with contempt Muslim culture and thought. Lord Macaulay, the author in 1835 of the famous "Minute on Education," which would influence the intellectual and cultural direction of South Asia, dismissed the entire corpus of Arabic literature – he threw in Sanskrit for good measure – as not equal to one European bookshelf. Even sensitive poets like Lord Alfred Tennyson dismissed the Orient in similar comparisons: "Better fifty years of Europe than a cycle of Cathay" (in "Locksley Hall," 1842).

Subjugated and humiliated, Muslim culture still showed flashes of tolerance. But the choices – and subsequent dilemmas – were tearing Muslims apart. Mirza Ghalib, Urdu literature's greatest poet, wrote in the middle of the 19th century: "My belief (Islam) constrains me while the acts of the non-believers attract me. The Kaaba (house of Islam) is behind me and the Church (the house of Christianity) in front."

The final crusade

Irrational hatred of others, the primordial urge to take revenge, the obsessive humiliation of women, and the declaration of holy war – this was familiar to us from the two crusades I have mentioned. However, the current crusade – because of our world's cultural complexities and the apocalyptic nature of our weapons – threatens to be the final round. It promises to resolve the unfinished business of subjugating or subduing Islam begun a thousand years ago.

Bush's notions of a crusade met, head on, those of bin Laden, who was already engaged in a holy war against America. Bin Laden, like many in the present generation of Muslim activists, is influenced by men like Sayyid Qutb, the Egyptian cleric executed by the state for treason in 1966 (see chapter 4, section i). Anti-Semitism, hatred of Israel and America, and a violent interpretation of Islam – the ideological stanchions that we recognize in many young Muslims today – were being set in place half a century ago. Muslim society has come a long way from the tolerant brotherhood of Rumi and the magnanimous chivalry of Saladin.

After September 2001 prominent Muslims – especially those living in or influenced by the West – denounced bin Laden and pronounced him and his politics "dead" (for example the Paris-based Amir Taheri in "A Perverter of Islam: Bin Laden and his Politics are dead," in the *International Herald Tribune*, July 12, 2002). They are wrong. Bin Laden has become a larger-than-life symbol of many things, including standing up to the West, to Muslims throughout the world. Muslim parents in their thousands are naming their sons Osama. Most important: Bin Laden has helped to trigger the present crusade.

As an idea, the present crusade is a powerful one

especially as it brings with it such deep historical, cultural, and religious memories. It is also a severely problematic and limited idea in its application. As enunciated by Bush, the philosophy of this crusade – "You are with us or against us" – appealed to as many as it repelled. Too many Muslim leaders, wined and dined in the capitals of the West, were vying with each other to sign up with Bush as his standard-bearers; many were loathed by their people for their blind obedience to America (Pakistanis contemptuously called Musharraf, "Busharraf"); many Western voices denounced Bush's campaign as it promised an open-ended, unending, and uncertain global conflict.

Because of the importance of cultural and intellectual ideas, the media, including film, are seen by both sides as key participants in the present crusade. The important voices for interfaith dialogue and understanding continue to speak up but find it difficult to be heard amid the noise.

After September 11 commentators on Islam were suddenly everywhere in the media. Much of what they had to say was racist and religiously prejudiced; it was hostility disguised as serious comment. Even the more scholarly voices were divided. Some, woefully few, wrote with sympathetic objectivity.[4] Some even talked of Islam as essentially a religion of peace and gave the historical example of Muslim Spain. They spoke of the grave misunderstanding between Islam and the West today. Others were more dominant and aggressive; they spoke of Islam as a terrorist religion and as the main threat to the West in the clash of civilizations.[5] The debate exacerbated the already existing divisions in what in the United States is called Middle East Studies (Kramer 2001).

There was open talk of the United States invading Muslim nations beyond Afghanistan. Iraq, Syria, Iran, Libya – even Saudi Arabia – these were discussed in the media as potential targets. Bush pointedly included Iraq and Iran as part of what he called an "Axis of Evil." Bin Laden, like the Cheshire cat, began to fade from the horizon as public enemy number one and was replaced by Saddam Hussein. Bush also emphasized the concepts of "pre-emptive strike" and "regime change" in his foreign policy. The world was alarmed at where and how all this would end.

Nelson Mandela, on the eve of the first anniversary of September 11, publicly rebuked the United States. It was, he said, creating "international chaos in international affairs." A few days later the German justice minister compared Bush to Hitler. This was absurd and unfair. It caused a furore, which exposed the complexity of the post-September world.

America's global war on terrorism had splintered into a dozen little battles that fed into local conflicts. Lines had become blurred. Confusion prevailed. There was a danger of the world descending into a Hobbesian nightmare; a war of all against all.

ii   The Sense of Muslim Siege

Never before in history, it appears, has there been a conjunction of factors that has allowed Muslims to kill and be killed on such a scale, with such extraordinary frequency, and in so many gruesome ways. If the actions of the hijackers had nothing to do with Islam, the causes and consequences of their actions will have everything to do with how and where Islam is going in the 21st century.

The day the 21st century began

Islam was at the heart of the events of September 11. On that extraordinary day, the President of the United States was on the run, zigzagging across America in Air Force One, escorted by F-16s and F-15s, until he returned to the capital late in the day to take charge. The stock exchanges were closed, all flights were suspended, emergency was declared in several states, and false alarms sent people scurrying for their lives. The scenes of panic on television would have seemed far-fetched in a Hollywood film.

But America began to recover quickly from the unprecedented carnage and mayhem; its native optimism struggled to reassert itself. The stars and stripes appeared everywhere, and interfaith dialogue was heard across the land. The president made a welcome visit to the Islamic Center in Washington DC, the city where I reside.

Dramatically, imperceptibly, the miasmic pall of uncertainty, of our lives being vulnerable and out of control, that hangs over much of the world now descended on Americans. People were aware that something had changed fundamentally. Like birds that vanish from the sky after a natural calamity the planes over Washington disappeared; the skies became eerily quiet except for the urgent sound of the helicopter, which added to the tension. When the flights resumed it was a relief to see something of normalcy return, but it was not the same.

In the weeks to come, the media stoked the sense of panic and even hysteria. Anthrax cases, fires in the subway, even a tremor in California – everything was instinctively being blamed on the "terrorists." This Pavlovian response would soon be embedded in the American psyche. A year later commentators without hesitation linked John Allen Muhammad, the deadly sniper who killed and wounded thirteen people in and around Washington DC, to Al-Qaeda even before he was caught and identified as an African-American convert to Islam.

War was declared on "terrorism" and in early October 2001 the bombing of Afghanistan began. In the highly charged atmosphere of the United States at the time no voice was raised to point out that not a single one of the nineteen hijackers was an Afghan; neither was bin Laden an Afghan. It appeared as if someone almost at random had to be selected and sacrificed to avenge September 11. Afghanistan was the most convenient choice at hand.

The war began with imprecise objectives and no stated duration; it suggested perils that could not be calibrated and unpredictable consequences. While the leaders of the Western alliance appeared bold and principled to their supporters they appeared reckless and impetuous to their critics.[6] Muslims protested in many parts of the world.

Wars are usually a consequence of the breakdown of communication between the protagonists. In this case it was a totally asymmetrical war in the most profound ways possible: the two different societies, one highly industrialized and world-dominating, the other still pre-industrial, impoverished, and tribal, spoke different languages and lived in different cultures. The only thing in common was the mutual incomprehension with which they viewed each other.

Government and media commentators pointed to Iraq, Syria, and Iran as other "terrorist" states and potential targets. Pakistan, which had nurtured and supported the Taliban, escaped the wrath of the Americans by hastily abandoning the Taliban and siding with the United States. This did not prevent many Americans from keeping a close and critical eye on Pakistan.

Bin Laden, in an extraordinary video broadcast on American television,[7] argued that this was a war between Islam and the West. The main grievances he listed struck a nerve in the mosques, shantytowns, and bazaars of the

Muslim world. The idea of Islam as an enemy was gaining ground in the West in spite of Western leaders insisting this was not true.

From the beginning, bin Laden, who had threatened the United States with mass terror on several occasions, was widely believed to have been the mastermind of the attacks. If a Peruvian or a Japanese cult stepped forward and claimed that it had organized the attacks, it would have been hard to accept. In the public mind Islam was to blame. Reports of the harassment of Muslims and attacks on mosques began almost immediately. In some cases, Sikhs were killed. They had been mistaken, because of their beards and turbans, for Muslims.

The years of negative press, news of hijacking or hostage-taking or honor killings, reinforced by big-budget Hollywood films like *True Lies*, *Executive Decision*, and *The Siege*, had conditioned the public to expect the worst from a civilization widely viewed as "terrorist," "fundamentalist," and "fanatic." Muslim "terrorists" had even featured in *The Simpsons*, one of the most popular television shows in America, when Mr Burns sold plutonium to terrorists wearing turbans, beards, and Arab headdress. In mainstream culture "Muslim" had become synonymous with "terrorist." The explosion in Oklahoma City six years earlier also had been blamed on Muslims, although as everyone now knows, it was the work of a white American man, Timothy McVeigh.

Observers described the hijackers as "extremists," "fundamentalists," and "terrorists," terms that told us little about the hijackers. Others described them as belonging to a cult, like the one headed by Jim Jones in 1970s' Guyana. That was perhaps getting nearer to the truth. But I suggest that McVeigh is the better comparison. The cause of Jim Jones was Jones himself. McVeigh believed he killed and died for a bigger cause. He had a distorted understanding of Christianity, nationalism, honor, and patriotism. A cold, calculating anger appeared to drive him.

Like McVeigh, the hijackers of September 11 defied conventional ideas of what motivates people to acts of violence. They came from middle-class backgrounds. They were educated in Western ways and familiar with the West and had everything to gain from living there. Their rage had as much to do with Islam as McVeigh's had to do with Christianity: very little.

Muslims were not helping their case after the attacks. Muslim guilt seemed to be confirmed for Americans as many Muslims refused to accept that the nineteen hijackers were even Muslim; they blamed the events of September 11 on a Jewish or Christian conspiracy against Islam. Americans reacted with disbelief to the jubilation they saw in parts of the Muslim world, where people distributed sweets and chanted slogans against America.

> Egypt's privately owned "independent" press also celebrated the terrorist attacks against the United States: "Millions across the world shouted in joy: America was hit!" wrote *Al-Maydan* (an independent weekly) columnist Dr. Nabil Farouq. "This call expressed the sentiments of millions across the world, whom the American master had treated with tyranny, arrogance, bullying, conceit, deceit, and bad taste – like every bully whom no one has yet put in his place." (Pearson and Clark 2002: 374)

The insensitivity of the Muslim reaction rubbed salt into American wounds and, for some Americans, removed any doubts about taking revenge. Few recognized the humiliation, terror, and neurosis in Muslim society from the decades of emotional and physical violence to which they had been subjected; fewer still understood that many Muslims blamed America for their plight. The idea of

Islam set on a collision course with America triumphed
over any other ideas of global peace and dialogue.

The Muslim world seems to be torn between those who
would shake heaven and earth to get a green card and
become Americans and those who would shake heaven
and earth to destroy or damage Americans. For both
groups, the United States is the most important, most
visible, and most powerful representation of all that is
good or bad in Western civilization.

The rising tide of Islamophobia

The rising tide of Islamophobia encouraged incidents
against Muslims, and these incidents further fed the Islamophobia. For evidence, Muslims needed only to look at
the shocking killings of some Muslims in the West, where
many were picked up for interrogation and many others
felt harried and humiliated. Several Muslim charities were
shut down; women wearing the *hijab* were harassed. Fox
television commentator Bill O'Reilly equated the holy
book of the Muslims, the Quran, to Hitler's *Mein Kampf*;
so much for the channel's self-description as offering "fair
and balanced" coverage.

The fear of and loathing against Islam were even more
pronounced in religious circles. The Reverend Jerry Vines,
former leader of the Southern Baptist Convention, the
largest Protestant denomination in the United States,
denounced the Prophet of Islam as a "demon-possessed
paedophile." To the Reverend Jerry Falwell the Prophet
was a "terrorist." The Reverend Franklin Graham, who
offered the invocation at Bush's inauguration, called Islam
"a very wicked and evil religion." Islam's God was not the
God of Christianity, declared Graham, the son of Billy
Graham. Pat Robertson said much the same thing.

The marginal, obscure, and even academically dubious

work of a group of so-called "new historians" of Islam, who sought to undermine the foundations of Islam, was further cause for alarm. They suggested that the Prophet was not a real historical figure and that the Quran was patched together centuries after his supposed death in 632 AD. Most controversially, these researchers argued "The religion may be best understood as a heretical branch of rabbinical Judaism" (see "The Great Koran Contrick" by Martin Bright in *New Statesman*, December 10, 2001: 25).

Certain Christian groups launched an offensive to "eliminate Islam" altogether (see "False Prophets: Inside the Evangelical Christian Movement That Aims to Eliminate Islam" by Barry Yeoman in *Mother Jones*, June 2002). Richard Lowry, the editor of *National Review*, created a storm of controversy when he came up with a "final" solution to the Muslim problem: "Nuke Mecca" and force the remaining Muslims to accept Christianity (see National Review Online, "The Corner", March 7, 2002).

Modern communications made it possible for intelligence agencies throughout the world to work together efficiently in hunting down those they were calling terrorists. On that list were some people legitimately demanding their rights but now seen by governments as troublemakers.[8]

After September 11, local authorities could pick up any young Muslim male anywhere in the world without questions being asked. On the contrary, the only power that mattered, the United States, was seen as aggressively anxious to pursue "terrorists" wherever they lived. It did not take long for those who wished to discourage their Muslim populations from demanding an entire range of rights to figure out that if they labeled the Muslims "terrorists" they could request support and even aid from Washington. Sure enough American troops were soon deployed against a variety of local Muslim groups who

normally would have looked to Washington for help as
they faced human rights violations. The Chechens in
Russia are an example. The Uigar in China, the Kashmiris
in India, the Palestinians in Israel – after September theirs
became a lost cause. The ongoing suppression of their
population had aspects of genocide. No one appeared to
be able to do much to stop the slaughter. No one appeared
to be really interested.

As a result too many Muslim civilians are being killed
and too many homes being blown up across the world
with impunity. Too many people are being picked up and
humiliated or tortured. Many simply disappear. There is
a great deal of anger among ordinary Muslims at the
injustices perpetrated against them that they see on their
television sets and within their own societies.

Muslims have seen how for half a century UN resolu-
tions aimed at alleviating the suffering of Palestinians and
Kashmiris were ignored. Yet, conversely, the UN was
swift to act against Muslim states like Iraq for their
transgressions.

It is the failure to redress the injustices of the Muslim
world that has caused the marginalization of the more
liberal, even secular, nationalist movements, which dominated the postcolonial era after the Second World War.
Only a generation ago, the rulers of the Muslim world
seemed to emphasize different aspects of modernity. They
talked of dams, highways, and industries. They avoided
talking of religion and tribes. Their failure has meant the
fading of the hopes and aspirations of the post-indepen-
dence period and the return to atavistic themes. Over the
last decades, but quickening in the last few years, such
shifts have encouraged among Muslims the emergence of
and support for men like bin Laden and their discourse of
violence.

The so-called "moderate" leaders supported by the

West, like Musharraf and Mubarak, continued to claim that the extremists instigated the increased unrest against their governments in the Muslim world after September 11. But while saying this, their police and security apparatus were firmly locking up anyone who would disagree with them at home. The Muslim Brotherhood in Egypt and the Jamaat-i-Islami in Pakistan, both mainstream parties, and no longer viewed as the extremists they were when they appeared on the political landscape half a century ago, were gagged and their leaders jailed. Ordinary people blamed the Americans for the increased repression.

In early October 2001, with the start of America's all-out "war on terrorism" in Afghanistan, and the subsequent hunt for "Muslim terrorists" elsewhere, the perception among Muslims began to grow that the "war on terrorism" was in fact "the war on Islam" (the title of Masud 2002, written by an American Muslim living in Washington DC). In the din few non-Muslims or Muslims were heeding the eternal message of the mystics of Islam – *sulh-i-kul* or "peace with all."

A new Andalusia?

Professor Tamara Sonn, president of the American Council for the Study of Islamic Societies, had several discussions with me before September 2001 in which she spoke of the United States as a new Andalusia – a tolerant society in which the great faiths live in harmony and contribute to a rich, mutually beneficial culture.[9] She was right. But after September, the freest, most welcoming country in the world for Muslims turned threatening to and suspicious of Muslim belief and practice.

America compromised its own idea of a democratic, pluralistic, and open society after September 11. The

voices that objected were too isolated to be heard clearly
(for example see "The Troubling New Face of America"
by Jimmy Carter in the *Washington Post*, September 5,
2002; also see Goldberg, Goldberg and Greenwald 2002;
Cole, Dempsey and Goldberg 2002). There were stories
of Muslims, or what the media called men of "Middle
Eastern appearance," being detained or disappearing. It
was alleged that some even died in interrogation. Racial
profiling in the United States meant that Muslims could
be interrogated, questioned, and deported if necessary
with little or no outcry in the media. In any case, polls
showed that about 80 percent of Americans believed that
this was the way forward. Polls in the United States and
in some Muslim nations confirmed the distaste they had
for each other.

The general antipathy to Muslims was so great then
that when suspected Taliban and Al-Qaeda captives were
brought as prisoners to the United States army base at
Guantanamo Bay, Cuba – to the place known as Camp
X-ray – and some organizations raised the question of
rights, American media commentators responded by saying, "These are not prisoners of war and therefore, have
no rights." Noted legal personalities advocated the official
use of torture in dealing with Muslims (Dershowitz 2002).
Images of the prisoners shuffling about with shackles
binding wrists, ankles, and waists, with hoods on their
faces and masks on their mouths, guarded at all times by
burly-looking soldiers, and sleeping and living in six- by
eight-foot open-air cells, did not even stir the slightest
sympathy in societies that had talked so much about
human rights. Even the significance of the fact that the
beards of the Muslims were forcibly shaved did not regis-
ter in the public debate. The beard is the very symbol of
Islamic identity, revered in Muslim culture because of the
sayings and practice of the Prophet of Islam. That is why

when Mustafa Kemal Atatürk, the founder of Turkey, wished to identify something as essential to Islam, he launched a campaign to ban the beard. He was rejecting a core symbol of Islamic identity in an attempt to create a new identity. In the early part of the 21st century, the Americans were doing the same with impunity. Although the Americans were removing Islamic identity and Atatürk had set out to create a new identity, the effect was the same – a perceived assault on Islam.

Perhaps most disappointing was the American failure to see that Americans themselves were damaging something essential in their own society when they claimed that their treatment of the Afghan prisoners was to be compared to the Afghan treatment of Afghan prisoners. Unwittingly, they were comparing themselves to one of the most brutal regimes in modern times, a tribal, illiterate, and backward group. They were dismissing from their own history the struggle and evolution of modern political thought over the last three centuries. The practice of the midnight knock had arrived in the United States after having been discredited with the fall of the Soviet system, and people were not even aware of it. September 11 was changing the world in all sorts of unexpected ways.

Bush's exclusivist policy of "You are with us or against us" was creating complications abroad too. Bush demanded hard boundaries in societies where so many different identities – tribal, sectarian, national, and religious – over-lapped, merged, and lived side by side. It was difficult to locate where one identity ended and another one began. Where seeing nuances and living in gray areas was an established way of life, it was virtually impossible to change in the way Bush demanded.

Bush himself changed overnight in the minds of most Americans; his popularity ratings remained extraordinarily high after September. Americans now saw Bush as the simple but heroic Texan sheriff determined to protect his town and bring the villain to justice. Bush even spoke the language: he would take bin Laden "dead or alive"; bin Laden was a "slithering snake." But this was speaking to the anger of the people. There was no room for compassion and understanding. Like most people in the United States, Bush was coming to September 11 with an absolute idea of good and evil.

But it was not long before Bush became aware of the complexities of global society. A year after September 11, on November 7, 2002, he invited a group of Muslims, which included ambassadors, to have dinner with him at the White House during the holy month of Ramadan (see "Sighting of the Crescent Moon at the White House," my Religion News Service column dated November 20). In his brief welcome he emphasized the Abrahamic origins of Islam and that the war he was waging was "on a radical network of terrorists, not on a religion and not on a civilization." These were the two important points that needed to be made, and the president made them. I was privileged to be seated on his table and during the dinner he emphasized these points with conviction. He admitted that before September 11, like most Americans, he knew little about Islam. He was making determined efforts to understand Islam with compassion. Predictably, Muslim critics of the United States condemned Bush's initiative: "Uncle Toms dine with Uncle Sam," proclaimed *Ummah News* (November 27, 2002), one of the main media outlets of the mainly UK-based Hizb-ut-Tahrir, a prominent and active Muslim political organization which has vigorously supported Osama bin Laden (see chapters 4 and 5 below).

Another face of America

There is another face of America. Unfortunately it is not seen in the Muslim world. I saw it in Santa Fe in August 2002.

Santa Fe is an anthropologist's paradise. It is where three major cultures meet: Hispanic, Native American, and what people here call "Anglo." With its opera, museums, and art galleries, Santa Fe provides high culture for those who at the same time wish to be well away from the major cities of the country. Santa Fe attracts the rich and famous (the movie stars Gene Hackman and the late Greer Garson, for example), artists, scholars, and retired diplomats. Situated at 7,000 feet in the Rocky Mountains the town is also popular among skiers. Its name, "The Land of Enchantment," is well deserved.

While there, I saw Zia Drive and was taken aback. Why would Santa Fe honor the military dictator of Pakistan, General Zia-ul-Haq? The name of the road and the sun design on the state flag are influenced by the Native American Zia symbol, I was told, and had nothing to do with the general.

Santa Fe boasts the oldest mission church in the United States. It is also proud of the fact that long before it was the capital of New Mexico, it was made the capital of the northeastern province of New Spain in 1610; it is therefore the oldest capital city in the United States. The Palace of the Governors is the oldest public building in the United States.

The magnificent cathedral dedicated to St Francis of Assisi, which was founded when Santa Fe was declared the capital, dominates the center of the town. St Francis is an appropriate symbol for Santa Fe, as he symbolizes compassion and tolerance. I was told of a Judaic symbol at the entrance of the cathedral and went to look for it.

Indeed, at the entrance I found a triangle and in it, in Hebrew, "Yahweh," the word for God.

I was in Santa Fe at the invitation of Lee Berry on behalf of the Santa Fe Council on International Relations. Although the Council is one of many throughout the United States, for the small population of Santa Fe, its membership of 900 suggests a high level of participation.

The Council had arranged a Special Project on Islam which stretched over three days. It began with a public lecture that I delivered at the Greer Garson Theater at the College of Santa Fe. About 300 people participated. There were three other sessions on Islam. The questions were sharp and intelligent and revolved around Islam and its relations with the West: questions about women in Islam; the future of democracy in Islam; the role of the United States on the global stage and its relationship with the Muslim world. There was a general unease about where the war on terrorism was heading and where it would end.

I was constantly surprised at the level of sophistication and links to my own world: Lisl and Landt Dennis gave me their coffee-table book *Living in Morocco: Design from Casablanca to Marrakesh* (2001); Michael Hoyt, who had been a consul in the American Embassy in Karachi, presented me his *Captive in the Congo: A Consul's Return to the Heart of Darkness* (2000); and William Stewart, who had been a consul in Bombay and then a correspondent for *Time* magazine, gave me his columns which he writes for the *Santa Fe New Mexican*. He startled me at a reception by suddenly speaking to me in Urdu/Hindi, the languages of South Asia.

The warmth and welcome of these writers reflected the warmth and welcome I received from my host, Lee Berry, and his wife Sandy. A successful oil businessman, who held senior positions in London, Tokyo, Libya, and Indonesia, Lee symbolizes the spirit of the people I met in Santa Fe: the goodwill and generosity of friendship, the curiosity about other places and peoples, and active commitment to understanding. Unfortunately, this is the face of America that many people abroad do not see.

Lee introduced me to his twelve-year-old grandson Kyle, who studies at the prestigious Albuquerque Academy in Albuquerque. Harry Potter is overrated, he thought. He preferred *The Lord of the Rings*. Kyle's favorite subject is poetry. I asked him if he had read *If* by Rudyard Kipling. He hadn't. I recommended it. Lee reinforced my advice. I was confident that if Kyle got round to reading *If*, he would soon discover the wonderful adventures of *Kim*, also written by Kipling (1960; originally published in 1901). Although Kipling is out of fashion and rejected – sometimes unfairly – as imperialist, sexist, and racist, I believe *Kim* encourages a young readership to enter imaginatively into the lives of others. Kim, about the same age as Kyle, would help Kyle discover a world at once far and near: far because it is set in the distant lands of Afghanistan and the Indo-Pakistan subcontinent; near because America is now involved deeply in what Kipling called "The Great Game" in that part of the world. The discovery would assist the young American in appreciating that, in spite of our differences, we are all part of what Kim calls the same river of humanity.

2

What is Going Wrong?

What is going wrong with the Muslim community?[1] The
community or *ummah* is like the human body, the Prophet
had said: If one part is in pain the whole body is in pain.
After September 11, many parts of the Muslim body were
in pain. But Muslim leaders, to preserve their office,
appeared to have lost the capacity to respond effectively
to the challenges of the world and abandoned the idea of
pride, dignity, and honor. The leaders of most non-
Muslim countries were also seen as not caring for honor
either. Indeed it appeared we were living in a world
without honor: a post-honor world.

i Is it about Islam or is it Globalization?

Many scholars believe that Islam is on a collision course
with the West and is inherently inimical to the modern
age we live in (Armesto 1995; Fukuyama 1998;
Huntington 1993, 1996; Kepel 2002; Lewis 2002). I am
suggesting that Islamic societies – like other world cultures
influenced by traditional religions – are reacting to the
global transformations taking place. The reaction is a
mixture of anger, incomprehension, and violent hatred.
There is also an element of fascination with Western

modernity and therefore a seduction. The relationship between Islam and modernity is much more complex than the simplistic clash of civilizations theories would have us believe.

The notion of a clash of civilizations, in which Muslims are seen as the main opponents of the West, is a continuation of older ideas about Islam as a predatory civilization threatening the West.[2] The opposite idea is the dialogue of civilizations, introduced by President Muhammad Khatami of Iran in the United Nations[3] and supported by UN Secretary General Kofi Annan. Khatami's statement had a dramatic impact because his country is associated in Western minds with "terrorism" and "extremism" although this idea too is not entirely new.[4]

September 11 acted as a catalyst and exposed people's individual positions. Some like Dr George Carey, the Archbishop of Canterbury, renewed their initiatives on dialogue with vigor.[5] Others, like President Khatami, discouraged by the rebuff from President Bush who had called his country part of an "Axis of Evil," seemed to reject dialogue and adopted a strident anti-Western rhetoric. Muslims, feeling under siege, found it difficult to talk of dialogue with conviction.

Globalization

The sense of siege among Muslims did not occur abruptly after September 11. Nor is it restricted to Muslims. Over the last decades the pace and scale of political, cultural, and technological changes coming from the West have unsettled people living in traditional societies. There is a widespread feeling among them that too much change is taking place at too great a pace.

To describe the time we live in commentators use the concepts of globalization,[6] postmodernism,[7] post-emotionalism (Mestrovic 1996), post-human (Fukuyama 2002), the age of the triumph of capitalism (Fukuyama 1998), Westernization,[8] or even straightforward Americanization.[9] The definitions are debated and the concepts are sometimes used interchangeably.

Globalization in our time, by definition, temperament, and character, rests on certain interconnected features: Global communications, media, effectiveness of the multinationals, travel, tourism, and a generalized but shared awareness of the free flow of goods and capital which presupposes law and order; and also a sense of moving forward to a time of justice, equity, and well-being. For some captains of globalization it means ravaging the planet for resources and asserting the total triumph of capitalism; for others, an opportunity to spread economic prosperity; for the majority population it means dislocation and despair. Globalization is thus part-promise, part-reality, and part-imagination.

The underlying principle of globalization was that each of these features was related to the others; a collapse in one could affect them all. While communications and media remain intact, everything else has been adversely affected after the September attacks. Globalization lies wounded in the ruins of the World Trade Center and the Pentagon. Whether this is a fatal wound will depend on how world leaders react to it over time; their vision and strategy will determine the future of globalization.

Where rethinking and the restructuring of globalization were required, anger or confusion prevailed. Where long-term planning was required, short-term strategy dictated by immediate political pressures prevailed. Where the wisdom of sages needed to be heard to encourage dialogue and understanding, the shrill, angry, and infantile voices of leaders, almost all male, dominated the discussion.

Some commentators had already noted with pessimism the growing division between the industrialized, democratic, and affluent societies and those that are called developing societies. Indeed postmodernist gurus like Jean Baudrillard see the rich West confronting "the distress and catastrophe" of Africa, Asia (where the majority of the Muslim population lives), and Latin America in a mutually self-destructive and symbiotic relationship (1994: 69). Although globalization has brought many benefits for some regions in countries such as China and India, for most people in developing societies globalization is something akin to Armageddon. This is how Dr Mahathir Mohamad, the Prime Minister of Malaysia and a leading Muslim public intellectual, describes the impact of globalization: "Muslims and Muslim countries are faced with a tremendous and frightening challenge. Globalisation in the form that it takes now is a threat against us and our religion" (Mohamad 2001: 24).

Globalization has created confusion and despair: "I try very hard to be optimistic about the Muslims in the 21st century of the third millennium of the Christian Era," confesses Dr Mahathir (ibid: 44). "But I must admit that it is very difficult for me to be optimistic. I find few Muslims understand reality. They live in a make believe world where weakness is regarded as strength, where failures are regarded as successes."

Not only those living in Africa and Asia react with despair to globalization. As Kofi Annan, one of the world's leading diplomats and based in New York, wrote recently: "However, millions of people around the world experience globalization not as an agent of progress but as a disruptive force, almost hurricanelike in its ability to destroy lives, jobs, and traditions" ("Problems Without Passports," Kofi Annan, *Foreign Policy*, September/October 2002: 30). The processes of globalization which were already unsettling societies in different and sometimes unexpected ways created further tensions and distortions after the attacks on New York and Washington.

Although Muslims appear to be uncomfortable with globalization, the idea and practice of it are familiar in Muslim history. Islam's vision of the world is by definition global. There is neither East nor West for God (Surah 2: Verse 115). Islamic history has had long periods in which we recognize elements of what we today call globalization: societies living within different ethnic, geographic, and political boundaries, but speaking a language understood throughout, enjoying a common cultural sensibility, and recognizing the same overarching ethos in the world-view (see the masterly "Islamic" historians Albert Hourani (1991) and Marshall Hodgson (1974), for just how much globalization there once was in Islamic civilization). A man could travel from Granada in Europe to the Maghreb in North Africa, on to Cairo, then to the Arabian peninsula and from there to Baghdad across three continents, and still be in one familiar culture. Ibn Khaldun in the 14th century is just one example of someone who was able to live in these different places and still find himself in familiar cultural surroundings.

Another aspect from the past can provide inspiration for those of us searching history for examples of the dialogue of civilizations in a time of globalization. The Jews, Christians, and Muslims living in Spain until late in the 15th century created a rich cultural synthesis, each culture enriching the other, which resulted in literature, art, and architecture of high quality (Menocal 2000, 2002). The library in Cordoba had more books than all the other libraries of Europe put together. Key figures like Thomas Aquinas were influenced by Islamic thought. The Greeks were introduced to Europe via Muslim Spain and through the filter of Arabic. There were long periods of religious and cultural harmony. The influence of Muslim ideas, culture, and architecture on Europe was wide and deep. Then, Muslim society symbolized globalization.

Attacking globalization

The attacks on the seemingly impregnable and untouchable pillars of globalization in New York and Washington DC were the first major blow to globalization. Airlines tottered on the verge of bankruptcy and some collapsed. Enron, World Com, and Xerox, titanic multinationals, were exposed as riddled with massive corruption and mismanagement. Although their collapse was not linked to September 11 it fed into the deepening sense of crisis. Bush and Cheney with their business background, like that of many in their supporting teams, appeared vulnerable; it appeared that what was good for business was not after all good for America. The critics of Western capitalism gleefully detected the signs of an unraveling of globalization. They decried the greed and mendacity of those running the multinationals.

Globalization appears to challenge the primary forms of identity that surround most individuals: family – families are split as individuals leave home to look for employment or in response to a political or cultural situation, sometimes never to return; tribe[10] – sections of the tribe migrate to already swollen urban areas and, as the central genealogical principle of common descent weakens, begin the process of losing their identity; state – political and economic transformations affect every aspect of the state especially the idea of defined borders and in turn bring about changes in society; religion – the materialism and consumerism of globalization challenge the spiritual core of religion. When these various identities are weakened by globalization the nebulous but durable ideas of morality and justice, which represent God's order, assume exaggerated importance for the individual. That is why religion becomes not only a vehicle to interpret justice – usually translated as honor and revenge – but also a source of identity.

There were several widely held perceptions about globalization which contained an element of truth: that globalization is created and sustained to serve the American economy and politics; that at its heart globalization is morally bankrupt, seeking only material aggrandisement; that the consumerism shown on television in the advertisements, soaps, and documentaries about the rich and the famous represents normal average everyday life; that these Western media images invade homes throughout the world subverting local cultures and causing anger and frustration; that in its predatory drive to concentrate and consume wealth in North America, Americans, pampered and self-indulgent, will deplete the world's resources and condemn the majority population on the planet to lives of squalor. "Globalisation," sighs one of the pundits studying it, "is, at least empirically, not in and of itself a 'nice thing', in spite of certain indications of 'world progress'" (Robertson 1992: 6).

The stereotype of the United States is widespread. No matter that wave upon wave of the younger American generation is driven by an almost naive yet inspirational desire to create a better world (several of my American students from American University have gone abroad, to Palestine and China, hoping to make a difference); no matter that there are communities in the United States struggling for their rights; no matter that the belief in a better tomorrow and the wish to share the vision of an open democratic and tolerant society exists in most Americans.

For people living in the favelas of Brazil, Indonesia, or

Nigeria the images in *Dallas* and *Dynasty*, shown in re-runs, are reproductions of actual life in America. More contemporary pictures on TV advertising different products confirm the obsession with the physical and the superficial: For men – enhancing penis size and erection; for women – firming up breasts and buttocks; for everyone – drinks and fast foods, clothes, and cars. These are the images of consumerism, seducing and fascinating, revolting and angering, repelling and depressing.

The response in the rest of the world is a fascination with the United States (I want to be part of this) and a revulsion (I hate what I see as corrupt and corrupting and there is no hope of my ever being part of it). This revulsion is easily couched in moral terms. That is why the United States becomes the focus of anger. If the world is a global village then the United States has become the equivalent of the small and rich ruling elite of the village.

Stories of the extravagant living of the elite – including glimpses of how the fallen American CEOs lived – create anger and ridicule in the world. The Roman elite two thousand years ago, the Arab rulers in Baghdad a thousand years ago, the French aristocrats in Paris three hundred years ago may have lived lives of even greater consumerist extravagance. But high walls guarded their lives and people outside could only conjecture. Television has changed all that.

One of the most widely used symbols and caricatures of the irresistible American culture so widely associated with globalization is, of course, McDonald's. McDonald's represents myth, symbol, and ritual (see Kottak 2000: 466–8; also Barber 1995). In America, there is no escape from the golden arches. American University in Washington DC, where I teach, has situated a McDonald's on the main drive as you enter the campus. It is an admission of the power of the Big Mac. Abroad, too, McDonald's challenges culture at its very heart: In Casablanca a McDonald's overlooks the magnificent mosque built by the late King Hassan and known by his name; in Moscow, the golden arches face the statue of Pushkin; in Rome, McDonald's looks on the glorious Trevi fountain immortalized by "Three Coins in a Fountain"; in London it stares at Big Ben; in the heart of Cambridge it is situated a few yards from Trinity College where Isaac Newton, Francis Bacon, Alfred Tennyson, Muhammad Iqbal, and Jawaharlal Nehru studied.

As if to confirm its status as an instantly and globally recognized American symbol McDonald's became a target for deadly violence after September, most notably in Indonesia and India. Yet if you were to ask children in these places whether they would prefer a traditional, indigenous meal or a Big Mac the answer would invariably be the latter. Globalization is seen, as in the McDonald's example, as a steamroller from which there is no escape.

However, globalization can be turned on itself. Khomeini in the 1970s and bin Laden two decades later both used the processes of globalization skillfully: the media, Western technology, international recruits, transfer of funds, and the focus on the United States as the overarching enemy.

The connection between the negative aspects of globalization and the United States was clear in the minds of commentators in the Middle East after September:

Columnist Ali Al-Sayyed wrote in *Al-Ahram Al-Aarabi* weekly: "For many long years, America made many peoples in the world cry. It was always [America] that carried out the acts; now, acts are being carried out [against] it. A cook who concocts poison must one day also taste that poison! The world has discovered that the strength of the oppressed is great when the situation becomes unbearable.

The city of globalisation, with its economic, political, and military symbols, has collapsed, and the theory of globalisation will be buried with the establishment of the false coalition." (Pearson and Clark 2002: 373)

But bin Laden's actions had reversed the processes of globalization for Muslims. They now faced intractable problems at every border; they were checked and rechecked at airports; their business and financial concerns were repeatedly scrutinized; their beliefs and customs were viewed with suspicion and often ridiculed; and they were made to feel unwelcome in the community of world cultures.

"Risk society"

Scholars describe the period of history we live in as "a moment of gentle apocalypse" (Barthes 1989: xxii) and "an enigmatic and troubling postmodernity" (Foucault 1984: 39). After the attacks on New York and Washington, we are aware that the global transformations affecting local communities are neither "gentle" nor merely "troubling."

In the last decade or two we have seen how the global and the local, the high and the low, the past and the present, the sacred and the profane, the serious and the frivolous have been so bewilderingly juxtaposed and so instantly available to stimulate, confuse, and anger the individual. Violence is almost inevitable, the ethnic victim often at hand. Globally, the disillusioned children and inheritors of modernity live in uncertainty and aware of global changes.

It seemed that no one and no house was safe; not even the Queen at Buckingham Palace nor Prince Charles in St. James's. Both were burgled in their palaces. There was respect neither for property, nor the establishment, nor the aged. That is why sociologists looking for a term to describe what they see around them suggest that we are living in a "risk society" (title of Beck 1992; also see Ahmed 1992a; Ahmed and Donnan 1994; Ahmed and Shore 1995; Giddens 1990; Turner 1994); a "risk culture" (Giddens 1991: 3); or a "panic" culture (Kroker and Cook 1988). Ours is a "runaway world" (title of Giddens 2000).

It is a fallacy to assume that only traditional societies in Africa and Asia are uncomfortable with the speed and force of globalization. This element of uncertainty was illustrated in a television commercial I saw in 2000 for a wireless phone service in the United States. A young, successful executive is talking on a mobile phone when two muscular men dressed in overalls walk in and proceed to strip him of his clothes, lift up his swivel chair with him still in it, and hurl it out the window of his top-floor office. In the next scene the man wearing nothing but a cardboard box is standing in line waiting to buy a hamburger. The plight of the young man sums up both the realities and the mood of society. We live in a state of instability and uncertainty. In an instant we can be stripped of rank, status, wealth, and our sense of self, simply by choosing the wrong phone service.

ii   A Post-Honor World?

The processes of globalization have a direct bearing on ideas of honor. As traditional structures and values change and new ones are still to appear in any permanent way, globalization makes the individual uncertain and defensive and it exacerbates the sense of vulnerability. The individual lives in a state of what Durkheim called "anomie." I have suggested that such people respond by an excessive emphasis on group loyalty – or hyper-*asabiyya* – and create conditions for our post-honor society.

But it is not just the individual that feels threatened. The honor of the family, the group, the nation, and even the religion all seem threatened in various places and in unexpected ways. Everyone – from people living in the supreme hegemon, the United States, to the not yet born state of Palestine – feels vulnerable. Each accuses the other of knowing no honor, of being people of dishonor.

The mass media invade the most private rooms in homes throughout the world with new disturbing and threatening images. The news itself, instantly replayed, heightens the sense of anger and outrage, which feed into atavistic prejudices. People respond by defending the honor of their group, culture, or religion. In some cases revenge and martyrdom are one expression of the response. Too many people believe that while they are people of honor, others are not. They point to the dishonorable behavior of the other or to historical events to bolster their arguments. Through a distorted and even perverted logic, the notion of honor is applied to acts of violence, and innocent civilians are often the victims. Women are humiliated and even raped to assert honor (see chapter 4, section ii, "Veiled Truth: Women in Islam"). We can thus distinguish between honor as an idealistic and humanistic goal and as an exaggerated expression of group loyalty defined through violence against the other.

A matter of honor

Societies range from those that are highly industrialized such as in the United States, in which traditional ideas of honor are irrelevant or rejected – and hence they are post-honor – to those, at the other end of the spectrum, in which honor is still important and fiercely defended as in tribal Afghanistan. Other countries, like India, are somewhere in between, containing groups that aspire to be modern and also others that wish to emphasize tradition and honor.

Honor – or some understanding of it – is both universal and a continuous link with the past. Consider these varied and random examples. The Ten Commandments provide the basis for honor in societies influenced by the Judeo-Christian-Islamic traditions. The attempt to uphold the commandments – the honor of God, of the tribe, and of the family – has motivated individuals to acts both of nobility and barbarity. Popular novels and films like *The Four Feathers* convey the perception of honor in imperial Britain. Honor is central to the motto of the cadets at West Point, the elite officer-training college of the United States Army. In the United States, the myth of George Washington, the father of the American republic, chopping down a cherry tree represents the idea of the boy too honorable to lie. Societies not influenced by the Abrahamic tradition were also influenced by ideas of honor. Shakespeare chose the notion of honor, over economics and politics, with which to incite the Roman mob in *Julius Caesar*; the word appears several times in Mark Antony's speech after Caesar's murder. *Bushido*, the code of the Japanese samurai, rests on honor.

One of the earliest European descriptions of someone embodying honor comes from Geoffrey Chaucer's *The Canterbury Tales* (originally written in 1386 or 1387). Although Chaucer's cultural and political context is 14th-century Europe the ideal virtues of the Knight he describes – "Truth, honour, generousness and courtesy" (1977: 4) – were recognized as representing a person of honor until modern times. Many would argue that these virtues barely exist today. Worse: social and political life appears to be dominated by ideas of revenge and violence. One side of human behavior is dead; the other is overactive.

Today, notions of honor under attack remain an important discourse in political rhetoric and even behavior in much of the Muslim world. That is why *The Satanic Verses* controversy drew in Muslims from Bradford to Bombay. Muslims felt the Prophet of Islam and his wives had been dishonored. The title of the first chapter of Dr Mahathir Mohamad's important book is called "Muslim Honour and Dignity Under Assault" (Mohamad 2001: 9). A feeling of loss of honor is not new. What is new is the sense of apocalyptic disruption, which forces individuals to reconsider the interpretation of honor and invariably emphasize revenge as its simplest expression. At this point the discussion shifts from Dr Mahathir to bin Laden.

Bin Laden seized on the notion of honor in his attempts to rouse the Islamic world. He blamed corrupt Muslim rulers supported by the West, especially the United States, for robbing Muslims of their honor and dignity. The solution, he believed, was to strike violently at targets that would include civilians. Bin Laden was right in his first assumption – Muslims everywhere felt deprived of honor and dignity. He was partly right in his second assumption – there were after all many shortsighted and corrupt rulers who shared the blame for the plight of the Muslims. But bin Laden was entirely wrong in his third assumption. Islam, according to the Quran, could never justify the taking of a single innocent life.

The notion that the killing of Americans – and Jews – was justified in Islam was part of the distorted logic that led bin Laden to reinterpret Islam. As he himself said, "They rob us of our wealth and of our resources and of our oil. Our religion is under attack. They kill and murder our brothers. They compromise our honor and our dignity and dare we utter a single word of protest against the injustice, we are called terrorists" (Esposito 2002: 24). "For over half a century, Muslims in Palestine have been slaughtered and assaulted and robbed of their honor and of their property," he said (ibid: 23).

Muslims point out that men such as bin Laden make the valid point that Islam is not only about compassion and mercy but also about standing up for justice and against tyranny – whether in Palestine or Kashmir or Kosovo or Chechnya. Those Muslims who only empha-size the former are apologists and conceal a crucial aspect of their religion; they are without honor. That is why bin Laden's words and actions resonate in the Muslim world for ordinary people. It is this dynamic which provides the ferment in the Muslim world and which is not fully understood in the West.

Even before September 11 bin Laden had been warning the world of his intention to strike at America from his caves in Afghanistan. In several statements he used the word "honor" to justify his call for violence. When Amer-ica put pressure on the Taliban to hand over bin Laden, the Taliban replied that they could not do so: Tribal honor would not allow them.

Bush, in his highly charged addresses to his nation immediately after the attacks on America, clearly linked honor and the need to redeem it through revenge. For a while Bush embodied – and was seen as embodying by the majority of his people – the man of honor as he set about implementing his vision of redeeming honor through the foreign policy of the United States. Economic, geopolitical, and humanistic arguments were set aside for primordial ideas of revenge. The tribal society of Afghan-istan and the highly industrialized society of the United

States were on par in using the notions of honor and revenge.

In Pakistan, Musharraf claimed to have saved the honor of his nation, its *ghairat*, by siding with the Americans; but his critics called him *beghairat*, a man without honor. They said he had "sold out" to the Americans. Mosques and public places resounded with the cry of *beghairat*. To the people of Pakistan Musharraf had become a clone of Bush or "Busharraf." Musharraf was pointedly snubbed at the elections he organized late in 2002 by the massive support shown to the religious parties who denounced him and the Americans. The irony was that the Americans, with their characteristic short-term attention span in foreign policy dealings and natural impatience, soon tired of Musharraf. Within months he was being treated with contempt in the media. American news commentator Chris Matthews summed it up on his television show *Hardball* when he asked how can you trust Musharraf whose loyalty was based on "a buck in the pocket and a kick in the butt?"

In Israel, young Palestinians – including for the first time in the *intifada* girls barely in their teens – caused chaos in a series of deadly suicide bombings. Innocent women and children were killed in ordinary and everyday settings: a café or a wedding feast. People throughout the world were outraged and Jews rallied to defend the security of Israeli Jews at all costs. Not only security but also notions of identity and honor were invoked.

When Israeli troops responded by invading the West Bank and Gaza in the spring of 2002 and blew up buildings and civilians with a brutal intensity, young Palestinian men by the hundred were stripped, blindfolded, and tied up. The dishonor was unbearable. Arafat whose fortunes were at their lowest ebb ever in his shattered offices in Ramallah overnight became a symbol of honor for Arabs. Saudi princes and Iraqi leaders – traditional Arab foes – embraced each other in Beirut in a major conference and spoke of their humiliation and anger. Arafat, Bush, Saddam, bin Laden, the Taliban, the Palestinians, the Israelis, and the Saudis – in each and every case – were motivated by an understanding of the concept of honor.

The response of the Israeli army, which perceives itself as being under siege by the Arabs, has more than a hint of Masada; the Hindu mobs in Gujarat who killed, burned, and raped Muslims reflected the fury of a people wishing to assuage a thousand years of humiliation and conquest; the Serbs set up their rape and death camps to take revenge on Ottoman Turks and their victory at Kosovo. Muslim society, too, faces similar pressures and the need to adapt and change history. Today's suicide bombers are obviously reinterpreting Islamic belief based in the Quran. The power of the suicide bomber is in the contemporary impact he or she makes; their actions are kitsch, their oxygen provided by the media and the approbation of their community.

Arab honor

Arabs and Americans, journalists and diplomats, people from the developed world and the developing world were debating the definition of honor at every level after September 2001. Sometimes people seemed unaware of what they were debating. For example Dr Ghazi Al-Gosaibi, the Saudi ambassador to London, wrote a poem in *Al-Hayat* in April 2002 in praise of the 18-year-old Palestinian girl who blew herself up killing Israelis. In response, Thomas Friedman's column in the *New York Times* mocked him (April 24). Friedman could not understand

Al-Gosaibi's paean to martyrdom: "You died to honour God's word."

The key lay in the statement the young girl had recorded on video. She used the Arabic words for shame, dignity, and honor. She wished to shame the "sleeping" Arab leaders for their inaction in the face of the slaughter of the Palestinians on the West Bank. The mighty kings and generals were powerless to stop people being killed and property being destroyed. The girl also wished to reverse the terror felt by her people by striking terror into the hearts of the enemy.

Dr Al-Gosaibi understood the girl's pain; he is a poet. Friedman failed because he was too horrified and indignant at the consequences of her action to recognize the motive. This was a failure of cultural communication. The two interpretations could not have been more different: For one, her act was the ultimate sacrifice and symbol of honor; for the other it was murderous and dishonorable.

The massive demonstrations throughout the Muslim world after the suicide bombings meant that Muslim public opinion was enflamed. The cost had been high but the action appeared to have served its purpose.

Honor in Afghanistan and Pakistan

"Our honor has been outraged." The elders of Meerwala in south Punjab, Pakistan, demanded revenge. Abdul Shaqoor, an 11-year-old boy from an ethnic group that was considered lowly, had been seen walking with a girl from their tribe and they felt that their honor had been compromised. Members of their tribe kidnaped and sodomized Abdul Shaqoor.

Not content, on a sweltering day in June 2002, four tribesmen gang-raped Mukhtaran Bibi, the boy's 28-year-old sister, in broad daylight. The woman cried and pleaded. She reminded her tormentors that she taught the holy book, the Quran, to their children in their homes. Nothing worked. The community had gathered around the hut in which the rape was being committed and cheered it on. Mukhtaran Bibi was then paraded naked through the village. There was no one to protect her. The very people who should have prevented the crime, the leaders of the community, had themselves ordered it and participated in it. And this during military rule in Pakistan where the only justification for the general who had seized power was his promise that he would ensure law and order.

Sodomy, rape, and violence. Muslims violating Muslims. This is neither Islam nor traditional tribal custom. This is more than a social collapse; this is also a moral collapse.

The collapse in this case can be highlighted by contrasting it with the behavior not too long ago of other tribal people. The story of Ajab Khan is synonymous with honor among the Pukhtuns who live along the Pakistan–Afghanistan frontier (certain tribes soften the "kh" to "sh" and therefore say "Pushtun").

Ajab Khan's story is told under the title "Battles for Honour, God and Country" (Heston and Nasir undated); he is considered "the best-known hero of these stories from the North-West Frontier Province" (ibid: 265). Ajab Khan bridled under British imperial rule in the 1920s: "When Pukhtuns salute the British, it's like falcons being servants to crows – it makes me weep, for lions have become obedient to jackals" (ibid).

In April 1923, angry at what he perceived as an insult to his family in the Tribal Areas of the North-West Frontier Province, now part of Pakistan, Ajab Khan slipped into the British military cantonment in Kohat, killed the wife of a Major Ellis and kidnaped his daughter. The news made international headlines: *The Times* in London on April 16, 1923, carried a headline "Another Frontier Outrage: One Lady Killed and One Kidnapped" (ibid: 265); the *New York Times* on April 18 was more explicit: "Captive English Girl is Seen with Savages" (ibid: 265).

The British were outraged; it was still the High Noon of Empire. The idea of a female – Victorian attitudes toward women, including the placing of them on pedestals, still prevailed in British India – kidnaped by a tribesman was unthinkable. The regiments were marched up and down the Frontier Province and political officers were slipped into the Tribal Areas to bring back the girl at all costs. In the end the political officers succeeded.

The British sent a *jirga* (council of elders) to the Akhund Sahibzada, the local religious leader, and appealed on the basis of the Pukhtun code. (I heard the story from the son of the Akhund, in turn the religious leader, who became a friend of mine when I was Political Agent, Orakzai, in charge of the area in the 1970s.) Under *nanawati* or the code of welcoming those seeking redress no such appeal could go unheeded. Besides, great expenses were involved as the host had to feed the large visiting party and feed them well. In the end the Akhund drew up an agreement whereby honor all round was salvaged. Ajab Khan was sent into exile across the border into Afghanistan and lived a long life. His actions symbolize the upholding of honor in Pukhtun folklore. The British who recovered the girl and the tribesmen who helped in the process felt that their honor was upheld.

Ideas of honor, revenge, and martial valor dominate that land. Khushal Khan Khattak, one of the best-known Pukhtun poets, was driven by the notion of honor:

I despise the man who does not guide his life by honour.
The very word "honour" drives me mad. (Spain 1963: 63)

It was, after all, the Pukhtuns in Afghanistan who, in the mid-19th century, provided imperial Britain with one of its most chilling moments. The Grand Army of the Indus, which had entered Afghanistan as victors, had been decimated. The one surviving member, Dr Brydon, appeared on a cold January morning in 1842 in front of the Jalalabad garrison (Ahmed 1980: 92). He was half-crazed and riding a starved horse. In 1672, the Pukhtun tribesmen had wiped out an entire Mughal army in the Khyber Pass. Ten thousand soldiers had been killed and twenty thousand taken prisoner. The Mughal emperor's governor Amin Khan had barely survived with four others.

Significantly, Rudyard Kipling makes the Pukhtun the exception to his concept of "East" and "West" never meeting:

Oh, East is East, and West is West, and never the twain
    shall meet,
Till Earth and Sky stand presently at God's great
    Judgment Seat;
But there is neither East nor West, Border, nor Breed,
    nor Birth,
When two strong men stand face to face, though they
    come from the ends of earth! ("The Ballad of East and
    West," 1892)

This obsession with honor has a destructive element, of which Pukhtuns themselves are aware. David Edwards provides interesting case studies from Afghanistan to show a man who pursues honor single-mindedly also damages himself in the process (1996; also see Ahmed 1976, 1980, 1991). In this well-known saying the Pukhtuns point out the costs of keeping up honor in mountainous areas where they are free to practice their codes of behavior: "Honour ate up the mountains and taxes ate up the plains" (Ahmed 1976: 71).

Post-honor president?

The actions of Monica Lewinsky, Bill Clinton, and bin Laden set the stage for September 11. Muslim reading of Clinton had much to do with their planning for September: If the President of the United States was a man without honor his people could not be different. It seems clear to me that bin Laden misread Bush on the basis of Clinton's behavior. To him all American presidents behaved in a feckless and dishonorable manner. It would be a costly blunder. Bush responded to the attacks on his nation as a man of honor bent on vengeance.

When Clinton admitted his affair with Lewinsky to the grand jury in Washington and retaliated for the attacks on the American embassies in East Africa by bombing Khartoum in Sudan and Khost in Afghanistan in 1998, he confirmed what is widely believed, to the point of caricature, about American society: that it has little to offer the world except sex and violence. It is significant that most of the subsequent attacks on him from the Muslim world seized upon this notion: Clinton was a man without honor, who was caught telling lies to his nation and, above all, to his family and his wife. A man who had no honor was not a worthy man and could not be trusted.

The response from the head of the Taliban in Afghanistan, Mullah Umar, summed it up: According to Islamic law, Clinton the adulterer deserved to be punished by being stoned to death. Had the mullah issued a *fatwa* to this effect we would have seen a complicated case of crossed international wires, as with the *fatwa* issued by

Ayatollah Khomeini against Rushdie for *The Satanic Verses*.

Private morals, public office

Significantly, in opinion polls the majority of Americans supported Clinton despite his alleged lies and deceit. That convinced the Muslim world that to Americans, economic prosperity was more important than honor and morality. The polls indicated the separation of Clinton's private morals from his public office. This is a division that cannot be accepted in a society in which honor is important. It was widely believed that while Lewinsky and Clinton were frolicking in the Oval Office, Yasser Arafat waited outside for an urgent meeting. Such stories suggested that immediate gratification appeared to be of higher priority to the president than the Middle East peace process.

Yet many Americans criticized Clinton's behavior as dishonorable and demanded his impeachment and removal. Kenneth Starr, the special prosecutor in the case against the Clintons, cost the taxpayer millions of dollars, precisely because Americans were concerned about the decorum and integrity of their highest official. A decade earlier, Democratic Senator Gary Hart was eliminated from the presidential race because of a photograph of him with a woman, not his wife, on his knee on a boat named *Monkey Business*.

The cynics said that Clinton was diverting America from his personal problems when he attacked Sudan and Afghanistan. Life was imitating art, they said, pointing to *Wag the Dog*, a film with a similar plot. Clinton was shifting his role from popular American president under pressure to popular commander-in-chief defending the nation against the terrorist threat and avenging the bombing of American embassies. With predictable alliteration, the world press was quick to link fellatio and fear of fundamentalism.

But this link was not just picked up by commentators in the West. While putting bin Laden on the front pages, the Muslim world also gave Lewinsky prominence as the *femme fatale* responsible for the president's downfall. The Muslim press saw in her confirmation of their eternally popular Jewish conspiracy theory. According to this, Lewinsky, herself a Jew, had been planted by the Jews to first ensnare and then expose Clinton so that Al Gore, who was reputed to be more pro-Israel than Clinton, would replace him.

The American missiles not only united Muslims – as for them there could be no two opinions about the flimsy evidence, the unprovoked nature of the attacks and indiscriminate killing – but also created a new instant hero in bin Laden. He was barely known before the incident but became a front-page figure after it. That gave a new and powerful lease of life to those Muslim groups that demanded confrontation with the West and were prepared to use violence. It was as if Clinton had calculated how to bring such groups to prominence. Bin Laden's growing popularity put the traditional allies of the United States – the leaders of Egypt and Pakistan for example – on the defensive.

Double standard

Muslim commentators pointed out that Clinton's missile attacks on Sudan and Afghanistan provided an example of Western double standards. They noted that while Radovan Karadzic and General Ratko Mladic in Bosnia roamed free despite their established links to the death and rape camps, the United States did not hurl missiles into their areas. Yet it was quick to retaliate against what it perceived as a terrorist threat when Muslims were involved.

Muslims noted, too, that when the bombs exploded in Omagh in Northern Ireland in August 1998 and the group known as the Real IRA claimed responsibility, the press did not denounce their religion. Yet for the bombings of the American embassies in the same month, the media spoke of "Islamic" terrorist attacks, thus equating a specific act with a religion. Indeed the very civilization of Islam was equated with terror. President Clinton's response in attacking two Muslim countries on two different continents shortly afterwards seemed to sum up this attitude and prejudice.

One is left asking the questions: Who were Clinton's advisers in his decision to attack Muslim countries? Did he have Islamic experts to advise him? What books on Islam did he read? Or did he get his information at least partly from television and films? Despite his statement on August 20 of that year that the cruise missiles "were not aimed against Islam," did he only see Muslims as terrorists and fanatics? Was his image of Islam a self-fulfilling prophecy? Similar questions could be asked about President Bush and Prime Minister Blair – who was so quick to defend both Clinton and Bush.

The uses of the past in creating honor

History is employed by a whole range of commentators, academics, and politicians to create or buttress an ethnic and religious sense of honor and, more importantly, to reclaim and reconstruct ethnic identity (Ahmed 1993b, 1993c, 1993d). Thus Kosovo in the Balkans, Jerusalem in the Middle East, or Ayodhya in India are not just neutral historical place-names. They are also deeply emotive and affective symbols of identity. They rally the community as they provide it with visible proof of the perfidious enemy by reviving bitter distant memories. In the mass media, such history translates into sentimentality and commercialization; it also becomes popular and accessible. In the vacuum caused by the collapse of the Grand Narratives like Communism, the indigenous becomes both relevant and inevitable. Honor, identity, and the media, the past and the future, the rise of what is called fundamentalism or revivalism all relate to the historical reference points.

Historical-religious mythology feeds the ethnic passions of Russians (like Vladimir Zhirinovsky) and Serbs (like Zeljko Raznatovic, widely known as Arkan), who talk of a Christian crusade, and of Jews and Muslims in the Middle East, and Hindus and Muslims in South Asia who view each other as enemies in a holy war. "God is with us," the faithful pronounce with utter conviction.

Religious hatred has a mimetic quality: The opposed groups mirror the hatred, rhetoric, and fears of each other. It makes everyone an outsider; and it makes everyone a target. Walker Connor contributed to the discussion by combining ethnicity and nationalism and used the term "ethnonationalism" (Connor 1993). He is right to underline the irrational and emotional wellsprings of ethnonationalism and its capacity to influence group behavior. Peter Loizos, in *The Heart Grown Bitter*, an anthropological account of Greek refugees in Cyprus, describes well the plight of the ethnically dispossessed (Loizos 1981).

It is this zeal that drove men in Bosnia to burn the sign of the cross onto the bodies of innocent Muslims and impale them in crucifixion (Goytisolo 1993; Yusuf 1993). Often, the first target in such cases is the village mosque. The destruction of these buildings is to be condemned on religious as well as architectural grounds, particularly as many of them are centuries old. Clearly, this is not in the spirit of Jesus. Rather, it is a crude ethnic justification for murder and violence.

Perhaps the most distressing aspect of religious conflict is the involvement of those who are considered the pillars of modern society, the doctors, lawyers, engineers, and writers (the Jewish mass murderer who killed about 50 Muslims and wounded 200 kneeling at prayer in Hebron in February 1994 was a medical doctor). But we need to be cautious here. Although religious loyalty tends to be a tidal wave which sweeps all before it, we can cite many courageous people precisely from this class who stand up to and expose the evil-doers in their own community: For example, Stjepan Mestrovic in the Balkans (Mestrovic, 1994); the Jewish women activists who authored a report (*Women for Women Political Prisoners*, 1989) on the situation of the Arab prisoners in Israel; Kanan Makiya in Iraq (Makiya 1993); and Dileep Padgaonkar in India (Padgaonkar 1993). His fellow Hindus in Bombay derisively dubbed Padgaonkar, Chief Editor of *The Times of India*, the Chief Editor of "The Times of Pakistan" when he attempted balanced reporting of the riots after Ayodhya and published the book *When Bombay Burned* (1993). Unfortunately these exceptions do not disprove the ethnic rule of religious conflict that members of the other group are considered aliens or enemies irrespective of their merits.

Although I point to the widespread nature and intensity of religious clashes, I do not mean to suggest it is characteristic of, or exclusive to, our age. Elimination, as in Bosnia, or segregation, as in the territories occupied by Israel, of the other (hated and weaker) group have been practiced in the past. The Reconquista and Inquisition in Spain and Glaubenskrieg in Germany, reaching a climax with the Nazi Holocaust, are examples of the former; *apartheid* in South Africa and the creation of Indian reservations in the United States, the latter.

Although honor is uplifting and noble in the abstract – whether slaying dragons to save virtuous maidens or helping old ladies cross the street – in practice it is never far from death and violence. Societies reach into the past and reinterpret events: Masada for Jews, Kosovo for Serbs, Ayodhya for Hindus symbolize communal tragedy and loss. The very names evoke deep passion and stir ideas of honor and revenge. They become a moral argument for our time. Group loyalty is exaggerated and group exclusivity becomes a dogma. So the perceived loss of honor centuries ago must now be wiped out through revenge on the putative descendants of the supposed antagonists. This is shaky history; it is also shaky theology.

In a post-honor world, passions will remain high as different codes clash. Understanding is therefore more crucial than ever before. Because of the economic, political, and cultural power of the United States, the rest of the world, however far-flung and remote, is now directly linked to Washington in a way that was inconceivable only a decade or two ago. It is crucial for Americans to begin to think of their responsibility in the post-honor world that is forming around us, and which they are helping to create.

3

Ibn Khaldun and
Social Cohesion

i The Khaldunian Breakdown

If we are indeed living in a post-honor world, how has this
come about? What factors are causing change in society
in order to allow a new way of thinking and behaving to
emerge? We are helped in the answers by the work of Ibn
Khaldun, especially his notion of *asabiyya* – group loyalty,
social cohesion, or solidarity. In this chapter I will point
to cause and effect: I will link the disintegration of *asabiyya* and its reformulation as hyper-*asabiyya* to the emergence of post-honor society.

The father of sociology

Bin Laden is a household name in the West, where,
unfortunately, the names of important Muslim scholars
are less well known. When I talk of Ibn Khaldun Americans usually ask: Who is he? An oil sheikh? An Arab
minister? Another "terrorist"? Any links to bin Laden?
Even the scholars who have heard of Ibn Khaldun may
well ask: How is he relevant to problems of the 21st
century?

I shall attempt to answer. The noted historian Arnold
Toynbee, appreciating the scope and scale of Ibn Khal-

dun's work, called it "undoubtedly the greatest work of its kind that has ever yet been created by any mind in any time or place" (Ibn Khaldun 1969: xiv). Not only is Ibn Khaldun generally recognized as the "father, or one of the fathers, of modern cultural history and social science" (Mahdi 1968: 56), influencing and shaping these disciplines into our time, but his work provides the intellectual point at which other world scholars connect in genuine appreciation.[1]

Ibn Khaldun's ideas foreshadow those of our own time. "Some of the central formulae of the modern age," I noted with an element of awe while attempting to discover the relationship of Muslim history to society over a decade ago, "are reflected in Ibn Khaldun's theories: Karl Marx's stages of human history, which provide the dynamics for the dialectics of conflict between groups; Max Weber's typology of leadership; Vilfredo Pareto's circulation of elites; and Ernest Gellner's pendulum swing theory of Islam, oscillating from an urban, formal literal tradition to a rural, informal and mystical one" (Ahmed 2002a: 101).

Indeed Emile Durkheim's concept of "mechanical" and "organic solidarity" reflects Ibn Khaldun's notion of *asabiyya*. It is *asabiyya* that is at the core of the Khaldunian understanding of society and we shall return to it. Durkheim, himself one of the founding fathers of modern social science, showed us how the collapse of solidarity leads to abnormal behavior. He called this "anomie." I will argue below that a kind of global anomie is what Muslim society is experiencing as a result of the breakdown of *asabiyya*.

As for Ibn Khaldun's ideas, it would have been inconceivable for Europeans in the 19th and early 20th century to think of a Muslim scholar who could write in terms of cause and effect, of drawing universal conclusions on the basis of observable phenomena, and one who could discuss the movement of societies in terms of social dynamics and not as a direct consequence of God's will. It is well to recall that Lord Macaulay's influential "Minute on Education" in 1835 dismissed the entire corpus of Arabic and Sanskrit learning with contempt. It was not a good time for Muslim scholarship.

We have to thank those individual scholars who worked long, lonely hours to salvage the Muslim scholars of the past; in this case, Franz Rosenthal who through his translation brought the writing of Ibn Khaldun to a large Western audience in the last half of the 20th century (Ibn Khaldun 1969). Unfortunately, the heat around the idea of "Orientalism" generated by Edward Said's thesis (1978) – that European writers studying the Orient just cannot appreciate Asian intellectual and artistic creativity and have a perverted and sinister agenda – has distracted from the acknowledgment that is due such scholars.

Said was right on one point: While the Orientalists illuminated Islamic civilization in some ways, they obfuscated its understanding in other ways. They saw Islam as one monolithic bloc. To them it was Islam versus Christianity; Western civilization versus Muslim civilization. The social dynamics within Islamic civilization, the interplay between tribe and state, between rural areas and urban centers, between the pulls of different sects, between the relationship of the leaders and their followers were not developed. That is why Norman Daniel writing in the Orientalist tradition in his acclaimed book *Islam and the West: The Making of an Image* (1960) makes only a passing reference to Ibn Khaldun in a footnote dismissing him as a polemicist. In contrast, Gellner, the renowned philosopher-anthropologist, places Ibn Khaldun at the center of his analysis of Islam (1981). Indeed he borrows from Khaldun to develop his own thesis. Gellner is able to penetrate to the heart of Muslim society. An anthropologist like Gellner looking at society and change is thus better equipped to deal with Islam than the Orientalist looking only at text and scripture.

There is a fundamental difference, however, between modern, Western sociologists and Ibn Khaldun. For all his "scientific" objectivity – and for many Muslims it is excessive – Ibn Khaldun still writes as a believer. There is a moral imperative in his interpretation of *asabiyya* as the organizing principle of society. Muslims see human beings as having been created to implement the vision of God on earth through their behavior and organization of society: Man is after all a "deputy" or "vicegerent" of God (Surah 2: Verse 30.) So *asabiyya* as an organizing principle is not "value-free."

"Social organisation," Ibn Khaldun wrote, "is necessary to the human species. Without it, the existence of human beings would be incomplete. God's desire to settle the world with human beings and to leave them as His representatives on earth would not materialise. This is the meaning of civilisation, the object of the science under discussion" (1969: 46). The social order thus reflects the moral order; the former cannot be in a state of collapse without suggesting a moral crisis.

Ibn Khaldun's methodological approach demonstrates intellectual confidence. Although based on sociology, Ibn Khaldun discussed in his analysis the impact of Greek philosophy on society (ibid: 373–5), the interpretation of dreams (ibid: 70–87), the influence of climate and food (ibid: 58–69), and the effect of the personality of the leader on the rise and fall of dynasties (ibid: 238–61). In his use of cross-cultural comparison, Arab, Berber, Turk, and Mongol groups would provide him the data for his theories. Besides, he was not writing as an isolated scholar but from the vantage point of a political actor in the history of his time. The rich material he gathered was the basis for his *Ilm al-umran* or "the science of culture or society."

"Ibn Khaldun's life," I wrote,

> forms a bridge, a transition, between the distinct phases of Muslim history which we are examining: the Arab dynasties in the tail-end of which – as in Umayyad Spain – he lived, and the great Muslim empires which would develop by the end of the century in which he died. His life also teaches us many things, confirming them for us in our own period: the uncertainty of politics; the fickleness of rulers; the abrupt changes of fortune, in jail one day, honoured the next; and finally, the supremacy of the ideal in the constant, unceasing, search for *ilm*, knowledge, and therefore the ultimate triumph of the human will and intellect against all odds. (Ahmed 2002a: 106)

All of us in the 21st century need to be grateful to Ibn Khaldun for reminding us of the lesson of "the human will and intellect."[2]

The breakdown of social cohesion

Ibn Khaldun's most widely known theory is that of *asabiyya*, which is at the core of social organization (the Arabic root has to do with loyalty and the cohesiveness of the group). *Asabiyya* binds groups together through a common language, culture, and code of behavior. When there is conscious approximation of behavior to the ideal, at the different levels of family, clan, tribe, and kingdom or nation, society functions normatively and is whole. With *asabiyya*, society fulfills its primary purpose to transmit with integrity its values and ideas to the next generation. *Asabiyya* is what traditional societies possess but which is broken down in urbanized society over a period of time.

Of course, Ibn Khaldun pointed out that certain civilized societies based in cities with developed social organization, arts, and crafts may take a long time to break down.

There was a dark side to Ibn Khaldun's theory. While *asabiyya* as an exclusivist principle worked for the majority of the group it could degenerate with changing conditions into tyranny for the minority. Besides, while the rise of a new order is full of hope, its eventual demise is both predictable and dispiriting. The inevitability of Ibn Khaldun's rhythm of history further confirms its inherent pessimism.

Ibn Khaldun famously suggested that rural and tribal peoples come down from the mountains to urban areas and dominate them, and four generations on, as they absorb the manners and values of urban life, they lose their special quality of social cohesion and become effete and therefore vulnerable to fresher invasions from the hills (1969: 123–42). This cyclical, if oversimplified, pattern of rise and fall held for centuries until the advent of European colonialism.[3] Even the disruptive force of European imperialism over the 19th and 20th centuries did not fully break the cycle.

Paradoxically, it was only after independence from the European colonial powers in the middle of the 20th century, when Muslim societies should have become stronger and more cohesive, that Ibn Khaldun's cycle began to be seriously challenged. It is now drying up at the source. Tribal and rural groups can no longer provide *asabiyya*; urban areas in any case are inimical to it. The result is loss of vigor and cohesion. Muslims everywhere are voicing their alarm at the breakdown of society. They know that something is going fundamentally wrong but are not sure why.

With the inherited colonial structures of administration, politics, and education disintegrating and new ones yet to supplant or consolidate them, and with old identities being challenged, Muslim society is in flux (see also Ahmed and Hart 1984 for *asabiyya* in tribes throughout the Muslim world). *Asabiyya* is at its weakest in these societies. Central and South Asian states provide us with examples.

Paradoxically, it is in those parts of the Muslim world where there is the unifying factor of cultural tradition, dynastic rule, or language, as, for example, in the states on the Arabian peninsula, that there is comparative stability. Paradoxically, these states are seen as reactionary by Muslims who want genuine democracy and as stagnant by those who want an Islamic state based on the pristine principles of the early egalitarian Islamic order. Nonetheless the unifying factors of tradition, dynasty, and language sustain *asabiyya*, which ensures continuity and stability in times of global change. This insight could lead to the incorrect conclusion that a society needs to be an oil kingdom to maintain *asabiyya*. This is not correct. On the contrary, as I have pointed out in earlier work, sudden affluence poses serious challenges to the integrity of tribal society (2002a).

Consequences of the breakdown of asabiyya and the perils of hyper-asabiyya

Americans asked after September 11, "Why do they hate us?" and thought they had the answers: "envy," "hatred," and "jealousy." We will look elsewhere for the answers. We will examine the reasons why *asabiyya* is collapsing and the consequences of the collapse – including the consequences to America.

Globalization is the easy target when looking around for something to blame for the problems of our world. But *asabiyya* was damaged from the mid-20th century onwards as a direct result of political developments. The creation of Pakistan and Israel, the revolution in Iran, the civil wars in Algeria, Afghanistan, and parts of Central Asia displaced and killed millions, split communities, and shattered families. A disproportionately high percentage of the refugees of the world – the truly dispossessed of our time – are from Muslim lands. Refugee camps are notorious breeding grounds for anger and despair. The young are consumed with a rage that derives from the memory of a home robbed. They have seen little but injustice and indifference in their lives.

Asabiyya is breaking down in the Muslim world and taking new and sometimes dangerous forms. A similar process can be identified within other traditional societies, which are non-Muslim. However I will focus on Muslim societies where *asabiyya* is collapsing for the following reasons: massive urbanization, dramatic demographic changes, a population explosion, large-scale migrations to the West, the gap between rich and poor (which is growing ominously), the widespread corruption and mismanagement of rulers, the rampant materialism coupled with the low premium on education, the crisis of identity, and, perhaps most significantly, new and often alien ideas and images, at once seductive and repellent, and instantly communicated from the West, ideas and images which challenge traditional values and customs. This process of breakdown is taking place at a time when a large percentage of the population in the Muslim world is young,[4] dangerously illiterate, mostly jobless, and therefore easily mobilized for radical change.[5] The consequence is the difficulty of creating a society based on justice, knowledge, and compassion. Most Muslims interpret this difficulty as denying their society honor and dignity. The conditions listed above distort and challenge the traditional understanding of *asabiyya* and create a new mutated, exaggerated, and often dangerous version of *asabiyya* or what I have termed hyper-*asabiyya*.

The collapse of *asabiyya* also implies the collapse of *adl*, justice, and *ihsan*, compassion and balance. The central Islamic concepts act as cement, holding *asabiyya* in place. When society itself begins to transform to the point where *adl* and *ihsan* are no longer recognized as central features of society, then one consequence is not only the disenchantment with the rulers (whose duty Muslims see as a God-given charter to enforce *adl* and *ihsan)* but also a disillusionment with society itself. The relationship between *adl* and *ihsan* and *asabiyya* is a close one and needs to be underlined.

The collapse of *asabiyya* also has sociological consequences. It creates conflict and violence in society. It sets one individual against another, one group against another. Along with the sociological consequences there is also a moral aspect. Conflict in society creates the two features of society that God warns against – *fitna* and *shar*, which are translated simply as chaos and conflict.

Those who represent *fitna* and *shar*, such as bin Laden, do so in defiance of God's vision of society. Bin Laden may have strong sociological and psychological reasons for creating *fitna* and *shar* but no theological ones. There is no reflection of God as Beneficent and Merciful in killing innocent civilians.

The Taliban in their original and natural sociological niche represented one form of *asabiyya* – a tribal society with social cohesion. Once, however, they moved out and assumed political power in Kabul, becoming rulers of a state, their lack of training and knowledge ensured their failure. Their exclusivist ideology, which had been their strength, now became their weakness. Equally important, it compromised their *asabiyya* and they practiced hyper-

asabiyya. Their innate disposition to place women and minorities in discrete categories was now exaggerated and grossly corrupted. Their treatment became brutal and violated the primary principles of *asabiyya*, leading to disintegration.

The Taliban are not the only example of hyper-*asabiyya*. In different ways other groups also reflect hyper-*asabiyya*: These include Muslim clerics in Iran, Jewish settlers on the West Bank, Serb militias in the Balkans, and Hindu groups in India. (If my analysis of anger and violence in the name of God appears far-fetched see the scholarly and alarming *Why the Nations Rage: Killing in the Name of God*, Catherwood 2002 and *When Religion Becomes Evil*, Kimball 2002).

To sum up: Although Islam insists on *adl* and the need to stand up and fight for *adl*, the ultimate aim is to create a society based in the notion of *ihsan* or compassion and balance and free of *fitna* and *shar*. With the collapse of *asabiyya* and creation of hyper-*asabiyya* neither *adl* nor *ihsan* is easy to attain, while society finds its expression through *fitna* and *shar*.

The difficulty of maintaining asabiyya in a non-Muslim land

Commentators estimate there may be more Muslims in India than in Pakistan, which has a population of about 145 million. They estimate populations because Muslim demography is an explosive political issue. We know that about one-third of the world's Muslims live as a minority. In the 21st century they are finding it difficult to maintain *asabiyya*, as we see in the case of India.

Mahatma Gandhi's vision of peace and harmony between communities lay in ashes in early 2002 in his home state of Gujarat (for a frightening, gloomy, and heart-rending commentary by one of India's leading writers see Arundhati Roy's article "Democracy: Who's She When She's at Home?" in *Outlook India*, magazine May 6, 2002). A prosperous state, Gujarat is dominated by the Hindu nationalist Bharatiya Janata Party, the BJP. Matters were building up to the savage rioting that began in late February 2002 and continued to claim lives months later. The rioting was linked to the determination of Hindus to build a temple dedicated to Lord Ram on the site of the demolished mosque in Ayodhya, an event that took place ten years ago and cost thousands of lives then. This time the violence was of a particularly virulent nature.

Take the case of Mr Ahsan Jafri. A loyal member of the Congress Party, he had worked hard as a member of parliament to reinforce India's secular position. But he was a Muslim. That was enough for the Hindu mob, ten thousand strong, to break into Jafri's house in the middle of the afternoon, beat him senseless, pour kerosene everywhere, set the house on fire, and then carry him into the streets. No one is sure whether Jafri was still alive when the mob decapitated him, poured paraffin on him, and set him ablaze. The mob then returned to the house, pulled out the rest of Jafri's family, including two small boys, and burned them to death.

Another group of Hindus turned the town's small brick mosque into a pile of rubble. In its place, they erected a shrine to the Hindu monkey god Hanuman. Yet another mob burned the Muslim-owned Moti Mahal Hotel. Others went looking for any signs of Islamic symbols. Not even cemeteries were spared. Quranic verses, displayed as headstones, were destroyed.

The savagery was not restricted to one town. It is estimated – and figures for such violence are always estimates – that more than 2,000 people were killed. The police kept to their familiar practice: turning up too late and doing too little.

This is how Roy described the gory events:

> Within hours of the Godhra outrage, the Vishwa Hindu Parishad (VHP) and the Bajrang Dal put into motion a meticulously planned pogrom against the Muslim community. Officially the number of dead is 800. Independent reports put the figure at well over 2,000. More than a hundred and fifty thousand people, driven from their homes, now live in refugee camps. Women were stripped, gang-raped, parents were bludgeoned to death in front of their children. Two hundred and forty dargahs and 180 masjids [mosques] were destroyed – in Ahmedabad the tomb of Wali Gujarati, the founder of the modern Urdu poem, was demolished and paved over in the course of a night. The tomb of the musician Ustad Faiyaz Ali Khan was desecrated and wreathed in burning tires. Arsonists burned and looted shops, homes, hotels, textile mills, buses and private cars. Hundreds of thousands have lost their jobs . . . Across Gujarat, thousands of people made up the mobs. They were armed with petrol bombs, guns, knives, swords and tridents. Apart from the VHP and Bajrang Dal's usual lumpen constituency, Dalits and Adivasis took part in the orgy. Middle-class people participated in the looting. (On one memorable occasion a family arrived in a Mitsubishi Lancer.) The leaders of the mob had computer-generated cadastral lists marking out Muslim homes, shops, businesses and even partnerships. They had mobile phones to coordinate the action. They had trucks loaded with thousands of gas cylinders, hoarded weeks in advance, which they used to blow up Muslim commercial establishments. They had not just police protection and police connivance, but also covering fire (ibid).

There was no remorse on the part of the perpetrators: "Muslims started the problem," said several Hindus in media interviews. "They should all leave India and live in Pakistan." The more aggressive Hindus chanted the slogan of the extremist religious parties: "For the Muslims, there is either the *qabaristan* (the cemetery) or Pakistan."

The violent aggressors overlooked the deep challenge their acts of inhumanity pose both to India's idea of itself as a modern, secular, liberal state and to Hinduism. The definition of Hinduism as compassionate and tolerant was itself breaking down. The rioting was triggered when Hindu worshipers returned from Ayodhya chanting slogans to Lord Ram and a Muslim mob set their train alight.

Lord Ram in Hindu mythology is a heroic and noble figure embodying the virtues of bravery, generosity, and compassion. He vanquished Ravana, the symbol of evil. Ram Raj or the Rule of Ram meant a time of justice and prosperity. The idea of Ram Raj was central to Gandhi's political vision. Ram's mythological ideal of a golden age helped Gandhi convert the notion of Hinduism from culture to politics and from private belief to public policy. To Gandhi, independence from the British meant "swaraj", a Vedic term implying reversion to the time of Ram Raj.

Not all Indian leaders supported Gandhi's evocation of Ram in modern politics. Jawaharlal Nehru, the first prime minister of India, was uncomfortable. He supported the idea of secularism and criticized Gandhi's propagation of the ideology of Ram Raj.

"I used to be troubled sometimes at the growth of this religious element in our politics, both on the Hindu and the Muslim side . . . Even some of Gandhiji's phrases sometimes jarred upon me – thus his frequent reference to Ram Raj as a golden age which was to return," Nehru complained in his autobiography (Nehru 1941: 72).

In the end Gandhi was devoured by the very forces he

had encouraged. He was shot dead by Nathuram Godse, a member of the RSS, an extremist Hindu group which Gandhi had compared to "Hitler's Nazis." Godse shot Gandhi because he believed Gandhi was sympathetic to the Muslims. When shot, Gandhi's last words were "Ram, Ram, Ram." Godse was killing Gandhi in the name of Ram; and in his death, Gandhi invoked Ram to call forth the ideals of nobility, compassion, and benevolence.

It is sobering to recall that in that very land Gandhi began his prayer meetings by reading from the holy books of Islam, Christianity, and Hinduism; that he fasted to prevent communal clashes. That is why they called him the Mahatma – the Great Soul. In time, Gandhi's saintliness would be acknowledged throughout the land, but his critics would also become more brazen. A man called Gandhi a "bastard *bania* [shopkeeper]" in a television interview in 1995. Gandhi was under fire from certain sections of the BJP. Gandhi had gone from being the "Magnificent Mahatma" to "Bastard Bania" in half a century.[6]

Hindu extremists were now offering Muslims all over India the standard choices of ethnic cleansing: absorption into Hinduism by accepting Lord Ram and becoming "Hindu Mohammedans" or expulsion (to Pakistan or Saudi Arabia or wherever) or to prepare for the destruction of life and property. From the Reconquista in Spain to the occupied territories in Palestine, subjugated minorities have confronted these dilemmas.

The transformation of what its devout and thoughtful followers see as a philosophic, humane, and universal religious tradition to a bazaar vehicle for ethnic hatred and political confrontation saddens many Hindus. The mosque at Ayodhya was destroyed in December 1992 and an orgy of killing followed all over India in which the paramilitary and security forces were later implicated. The world saw them on television idly standing by as the frenzied mob in Ayodhya went about its business. In Bombay mobs stopped men and forced them to drop their trousers; those circumcised were identified as Muslim and stabbed. We note the link between the media and politics, between the religious-cultural assertion of identity of one group and the persecution of another.

When millions of Hindus in India in the late 1980s and early 1990s formed a movement to demolish the mosque at Ayodhya and build a temple in its place they were referring to the time of the first Mughal Emperor Babar, who invaded India in the early 16th century. Indeed, the mosque was named for Babar. When it was demolished in 1992, millions celebrated. They had taken revenge for the dishonor caused by the Muslim conquerors who came to India from the 10th century onwards. To drive home the point of honor and revenge Muslims throughout India were harassed, humiliated, and in many cases killed – more than the number who died on September 11 in New York and Washington DC. Women were gang-raped. The rapes were filmed and videos sold in the bazaars.

Sex, lies, and videotape – this is how honor in our time is redeemed. The premeditated gang-rape of women belonging to a helpless minority, like the killings, was a far cry from notions of honor in Hindu society. I single out rape as, among Hindus, it is meant to be the most dishonorable of all crimes. Among the Rajput, a land-owning caste of northwest India, noblewomen committed *sati*, or suicide, to maintain the high moral ground when Muslims invaded their lands centuries ago. Muslim warriors did not know how to deal with this situation except through marriage. As a result, some of the Mughal emperors had Hindu wives. The synthesis of cultures was taking place at the core of society – the family.

There were also immediate and serious international repercussions to the riots after the destruction of the mosque in Ayodhya: Hindus were attacked and their temples destroyed in Pakistan and Bangladesh while angry mobs demanded a "holy war" against India in retaliation. In Britain, tension was created between the Hindu and Muslim communities and Hindu temples were damaged. The span of the responses confirms our other argument that to understand ethnic violence we need to keep its global context before us.

Although commentators singled out the BJP as the main culprit behind the ethnic violence, this is incorrect and misleading. Indeed elements in the Congress Party had long compromised on its secular position. Others too – influential opinion-makers such as bureaucrats, media commentators, academics – had been transformed and had abandoned their earlier secular neutrality on communal issues. Those who were dismayed by this trend were reduced to powerless spectators. But let us not make the mistake of the critics of the BJP by simplifying a complex phenomenon. Recent studies have indicated that different indices affect communal rioting in India (for an innovative study emphasizing social indices see Varshney 2002; for geopolitical analysis and its impact by a leading authority, see Cohen 2001).

Beneath every case of ethnic cleansing is layer upon layer of history and culture. The movement for a separate Muslim state, the creation of Pakistan (seen by many Hindus in a religious light, as sacrilege, as the division of Mother India itself), the wars between India and Pakistan, the perception of a threatening Islamic revivalism (in neighbors such as Pakistan and Bangladesh and also, of course, Iran), and the continuing problems of the Muslim minority in adjusting to the new realities of India all contribute to the ethnic suppuration (for one of the most penetrating and evocative books on Muslims in India see Dalrymple 1994).

Indeed as early as the 1930s, Madhav Sadashiv Golwalkar, one of the most influential Hindu ideologues, had held up Hitler as a model in dealing with minorities: If Hitler could come up with a final solution to the Jews in Germany then the Hindus ought to be able to do the same to the Muslims in India (1938). Hitler's subsequent genocide of the Jews seemed to inspire Golwalkar to greater religious hatred (1966). Hindu extremists even today continue to use the unsavory language of the Nazis. The tradition of virulent propaganda against Muslims disguised as scholarly research continues (Elst 1992; Oak 1990). Muslims in these works are depicted as drunken buffoons dishonoring Hindu women and smashing Hindu temples. These stereotypes feed into the mass media and neatly reinforce Hindu chauvinism, which is calculated to win the Hindu vote.

The battle for Ram is the battle for the soul of modern India. That is why it is so hotly contested. Unfortunately the battle spills into the persecution of minorities and the less privileged. These were the very people whom Gandhi fought for and who inspired him. Many fear that Gujarat may be the harbinger of things to come for Muslim minorities in the 21st century.

ii   The Man in the Iron Cage

Following Khaldunian logic, with *asabiyya* breaking down, society can no longer implement God's vision for human civilization. The crisis is compounded as the scholars of Islam, who could offer balanced advice and guidance, are in disarray. Muslims believe that those who possess *ilm* or knowledge best explain the idea of what God desires from us on earth. The Prophet's saying (*hadith*), "The death of a scholar is the death of knowledge," emphasizes the importance of scholarship.[7] Unfortunately, in the contemporary Muslim world scholars are silenced, humiliated, or chased out of their homes.

The ramifications for society are far-reaching. In the place of scholars advising, guiding, and criticizing the rulers of the day, we have the sycophants and the secret services. The wisdom, compassion, and learning of the former risk being replaced by the paranoia and neurosis of the latter. And to where do the scholars escape? To America or Europe. Yet it is popular to blame the West, to blame others, for conspiracies.

With the scholars driven out, or under pressure to remain silent, it is not surprising that the Muslim world's educational achievements are among the lowest in the world. Literacy figures are far from satisfactory, and for women they are alarming. As a result, women in the Muslim world are deprived of their inheritance and their rights, and the men in their families tell them that this is Islam.

With those scholars silenced who can provide objectivity within the Islamic tradition and resilience in times of change, other kinds of religious "scholars" – like the Taliban – working in a different tradition, interpret Islam narrowly. Islam for them has become a tool of repression. Women and minorities take the brunt. Political tyranny also grows unchecked, as the scholars are not at hand to comment and criticize.

Professor AbdulHamid AbuSulayman, the president of the International Institute of Islamic Thought and based in America, summed up the crisis to me: "The Muslim scholar is either caught between the ignorant mullahs threatening him with *Jahannum* (hell) or the corrupt rulers threatening him with jail" (AbuSulayman 1993a and 1993b). This choice – *Jahannum* versus jail – was the direct consequence of the collapse of *asabiyya*.

Jahannum *or jail: the fate of the Muslim scholar*

The picture of Professor Saad Eddin Ibrahim, the noted Egyptian scholar and director of the Ibn Khaldun Center in Cairo, on the cover of the *New York Times Magazine* (June 17, 2001) behind bars and in a cage was a powerful metaphor for Muslim scholarship in the world today. Professor Ibrahim, like Anwar Ibrahim in Malaysia, was in jail charged with embezzlement and spying for the West – standard charges across the two continents; Anwar Ibrahim was also charged with homosexuality. Both are critical thinkers actively involved in their societies.

They are not alone in being persecuted. An entire generation of scholars has been eliminated in countries like Algeria and Afghanistan. (For a detailed analysis of persecuted scholars see Abdelkader 2000.) There is another category of scholars on the run. Writers like Salman Rushdie and Khalid Duran (see Duran 2001), both in hiding for fear of their lives, form a distinct category because they have a Muslim background. They are seen as beyond the pale by most Muslims and evoke extreme hostility.

Where then is the geographical center of the rethinking, or even thinking, on Islam? The Muslim countries themselves have proved barren. There are some notable new centers of learning and research in the Muslim world. Those in Cairo, Amman, Islamabad, and Kuala Lumpur are worth mentioning. Some of them have excellent physical facilities. Some produce competent journals and even books that are locally read by scholars. However, they have failed to produce either major international works or scholars or intellectual movements. In that sense, in spite of the resources at their disposal, their failure is spectacular. It can only be explained by the failure of the society within which they live and the general sense of despair, disillusionment, and discouragement.

Take Pakistan, a relatively moderate Muslim nation. Scholars – Abdullah Yusuf Ali, the translator of the Quran (see below), Rahmat Ali, who gave Pakistan its name, Fazlur Rahman, the eminent Islamic scholar, and Abdus Salam, the only Nobel Prize winner of Pakistan[8] – were encouraged to leave by the intolerant and the ignorant or *jahil*. Those who wished to return to Pakistan and contribute, such as Mahbub-ul-Haq and Eqbal Ahmed, died frustrated and broken-hearted. A Muslim scholar puts the case forcefully: "It is not an easy task for any conscientious Muslim intellectual in the Muslim world or in the West to undertake this critical task without endangering his or her life" (Sachedina 2001: 149, n. 38; see also Ahmed and Rosen 2001). The case of Abdullah Yusuf Ali is worth examining further.

The man who translated the Quran

"The winter of 1953 was a harsh one in Britain," writes the biographer of Abdullah Yusuf Ali (Sherif 1994: vii).

> On Wednesday 9 December, a confused old man was found out of doors, sitting on the steps of a house in Westminster. The police took him to Westminster Hospital. He was discharged the following day to a London County Council home for the elderly in Dovehouse Street, Chelsea. He suffered a heart attack on 10 December and was rushed to St Stephen's Hospital in Fulham. Three hours after admission he died . . . So, in these enigmatic circumstances, ended the remarkable life of Abdullah Yusuf Ali, at the age of 81. (ibid)

Before Ali died, the Pakistan High Commissioner in London had written to the Prime Minister of Pakistan:

> My dear Mohammed Ali: I write to you in connection with a person known to me and respected not only by Muslim youth of my time, but by Muslims the world over for the great services he has rendered to Islam during his lifetime and for his translation of the Holy Qur'an into English. His name is Abdullah Yusuf Ali who was born 81 years ago. In the 'Who's Who' of 1953, on page 36, one whole column is devoted to his qualifications, activities and achievements. I have just now learned that this venerable old man is in financial straits. He has been found sitting in Trafalgar Square in tattered clothes on a suitcase having no money in his pocket. He has been taken to the London County Council Poor Home and we have been informed of his condition. (ibid: 139–40)

The government of Pakistan chose not to do anything. But Yusuf Ali lives on in his translation. His translation of the holy Quran in its first edition ran into 30 instalments and was printed between 1934 and 1937 in Lahore. It was consolidated into three volumes in the second edition. Yusuf Ali was a popular speaker invited to lecture in different parts of the world at a time when there were few globe-trotting Muslim scholars. On his Canadian tour in 1938 he formally inaugurated the mosque at Edmonton, reputed to be the first in Canada. But his heart was broken when his wife not only committed adultery but the case became public and she conceived a child which was not his. The anguish is reflected in his commentary accompanying the Quranic translation.

Although the Muslim world appreciates and continues to read Yusuf Ali's translation, in his lifetime he faced and was hurt by Muslim jealousies (see chapter 5, section i, for contemporary Muslim malice). He wrote: "I had not imagined that so much human jealousy, misunderstanding and painful misrepresentation should pursue one who seeks no worldly gain and pretends to be no dogmatic authority" (ibid: 109). Yusuf Ali despaired of Muslim disunity, a point so relevant to Muslims today. While commenting on Muslims as a minority he wrote: "Muslims had many lessons to learn in how to deport themselves as a minority: The French Canadians were well organized 'both in church and state' while 'our Muslims are disorganized and individualistic' " (ibid: 129).

Yusuf Ali's last years and the manner of his death are a sad comment on how Muslims treat their great scholars – with indifference and neglect. We know that during their lifetimes even the best-known Muslim scholars and poets, like Allama Iqbal and Mirza Ghalib, were often one step from poverty. We have their letters to the nawabs and feudal lords requesting money for survival. So the death of Yusuf Ali should come as no surprise except in that it is especially poignant because it took place in a foreign land.

Muslim scholars abroad

It is notable that perhaps the best-known Muslim scholars have succeeded only once they have escaped from the Muslim lands to the West: Fazlur Rahman (of Pakistan) came to the University of Chicago; Muhammad Ayoob (of Lebanon) and Ismail al-Faruqi (of Palestine) to Temple University in Pennsylvania; Muhammad Arkoun (of Algeria) to the Sorbonne in Paris. Many scholars who are based in Muslim lands have produced their most creative work in the West: Khurshid Ahmad (Pakistan) at the Islamic Foundation in Leicester, UK, and Ali Ashraf (Bangladesh) at the Islamic Academy in Cambridge, UK, come to mind. It is also noteworthy that perhaps the best-known Islamic journals are produced in the West: *The*

American Journal of Islamic Social Sciences (USA) and *The Muslim World Book Review*, *The Muslim Educational Quarterly* and *Impact* (UK).

The problems of the Muslim scholars would not leave me even in the States. In January 2001 Dr. Sohail Zaidi, a distinguished Pakistani scientist in the Mechanical and Aerospace Engineering Department at Princeton University, shared with me the enduring image of education in his homeland. It was a memory from his youth and it was seared in his mind. He recalled that he lived in a remote part of Pakistan and his school was at a distance. He would journey from his home to school every day by train. The train was always full, so usually he had to fight his way into the compartments. He recalled one day, just before his exams, gathering his notes and books under his arm and jumping on to the moving train. He clung on to the railing with one hand while holding onto his treasure of knowledge with the other. To his great dismay the people inside the compartment refused to open the door to let him in although they could see his plight. He pleaded with them. They ignored him. The train now began to pick up speed. He had to decide whether to throw his books and notes away or save his life. He saved his life. All those years later he recounted the story with bitterness; his society had no respect for learning or books.

The scholar was aware that because he did not belong to an elite Pakistani family he was denied access to better schools. He was also aware that, because he was a refugee from India, he would find it difficult to work in the administrative and political structure of Pakistan, which was weighted heavily against people like him. Yet what burned in him was an obsession to acquire knowledge. He had accumulated degree after degree in Western universities.

Western universities had been good to him. He

migrated to the United States. Pakistan's loss was the gain of the West, and another scholar was lost to the Muslim world. His story reflects the indifference to *ilm* or knowledge that characterizes Muslim society. This is particularly poignant as *ilm* is so highly treasured in Islam itself.

One year later I confronted the case of another Muslim scholar. This one had stayed on in Pakistan and he wrote me a letter.

A letter from the death cell

It is not every day that I get a letter from the death cell, Central Jail, Rawalpindi, in Pakistan. As any Pakistani would be, I was aware that Central Jail was where the most popular elected prime minister of Pakistan, Zulfiqar Ali Bhutto, was sent to the gallows in 1979. Beaten, deprived of sleep, and denied medical facilities, Bhutto's last days were miserable. His execution left a permanent impression on the Pakistani psyche. It also polarized the society, which has not yet fully recovered.

The letter was dated April 15, 2002. Addressed to a Pakistani colleague at the university and myself, it was written in a clear and neat hand. The writer was Dr Mohammed Younas Sheikh.

The name instantly rang a bell. Some months earlier I had written an article, "Islam, Academe, and Freedom of the Mind", with Lawrence Rosen of Princeton University for *The Chronicle of Higher Education* (November 2, 2001). We had argued that too many scholars were humiliated, harassed, and silenced in the Muslim world. Many escaped abroad. The consequences for society were devastating. A vacuum formed in society that was filled by the secret services manipulating information. Society was pushed further toward intolerance.

In *The Chronicle* article we had mentioned Dr Sheikh:

"In Islamabad, a professor at a medical college this year was found guilty of blasphemy and sentenced to death, after students complained about him to the local religious leader." Neither of us had met Dr Sheikh but we gave his example to illustrate a dangerous trend in the Muslim world:

> Professors, particularly in the liberal arts, are often cowed by their own students into silence, both in their teaching and in their writing. Like some post-modernist gone mad, the student of literature may see fiction as nothing but the expression of the writer's politics, while the science student is not concerned with questioning fundamentals, but with applying technologies to religious and political ends. The results for intellectuals range from a denial of the finest traditions of open debate to working in an environment of omnipresent threat. (ibid)

For someone in the death cell, Dr Sheikh's letter was remarkably collected. There was no self-pity or hysteria. Dr Sheikh complained about the Blasphemy Law in Pakistan which, he said, "is wide open to abuse, through and by the miscreant mullahs for political, repressive and vindictive purposes on the pretext of undefined blasphemy . . . its abuse is a rising wave of aggressive ignorance, incivility and intolerance as well as the medieval theocratic darkness."

Dr Sheikh noted that his trial was held *in camera* inside the jail. "The learned court . . . succumbed to threats and after dubious in camera proceedings sentenced me to the death penalty under the said Blasphemy Law 295/C PPC without good evidence . . . even my solicitors were harassed with a *fatwa* (bull) of apostasy and they were threatened with the lives of their children."

The letter requested that we bring the case to the notice of General Pervez Musharraf, the president, so that he could "repeal this notorious and fascist Blasphemy Law."

Musharraf had assumed power after a military coup in late 1999. His instincts were to modernize Pakistan. He had made a small improvement in the Blasphemy Law early in 2000. But under pressure he had backed down within a few weeks and Pakistan was back to square one.

On one level, the argument for the Blasphemy Law is strong. Under it, words or acts of blasphemy against the Prophet of Islam are prohibited in Pakistan. After all, in a country that is 95 percent Muslim, only an insane man would blaspheme the Prophet. On another level, the law is used frequently for political or even economic reasons. An argument over property between a Muslim and his Christian neighbor can easily end with the Muslim accusing the Christian of blaspheming against the Prophet. Once the wheels of justice begin to move, there is little hope of escape for the accused. The media play up every such case as news and ensure certain hysteria; all this acts as pressure on the administration.

Most Pakistanis will invariably side with the administration. If they perceive their culture as being under attack they will close ranks. That is why, except for some enlightened Pakistanis from the cities, there is little real clamor to remove that law.

But Musharraf cannot avoid taking a bold stand in the case of Dr Sheikh. Either Musharraf is for modernizing Pakistan or he is not. And if the former, he must intervene. Dr Sheikh's situation is a test case for the kind of Pakistan Musharraf wants. To those who will argue with Musharraf against this line of thinking on Islamic grounds I would remind him to read the passages in the Quran which emphasize compassion and mercy as the greatest qualities of the ruler. (In hoping to bring the plight of Dr Sheikh to the world I wrote "Pakistan's Blasphemy Law: Words Fail Me," *Washington Post*, May 19, 2002.)

Pakistan has moved a long way from the time of my

education in the 1950s when there appeared to be more tolerance in society.

A Catholic school in Pakistan: sins of the father

I have a confession to make. I was educated at a Catholic boarding school for boys. For me, a Muslim, to write favorably of Catholic priests may sound like a paradox. My school was a paradox: a Catholic school in the north of Pakistan, a country that is almost entirely Muslim. The school was situated in the hill-station of Abbottabad.

Let me disabuse those who expect Catholic priests in a Muslim country to be fanatical tyrants. My earliest memories going back half a century to the 1950s are of understanding and generally compassionate teachers. Even as a boy, I wondered at the immense sacrifices that these priests had made. No family, no leisure, no personal indulgences; an austere regimen and the need always to be cheerful.

Although one or two fathers behaved as though the first crusades were not quite over, the others became surrogate parents. In the absence of our fathers for the long academic year these priests became what we addressed them as – "fathers." They were also role models. Their frugality and austerity, their good humor and compassion and general sense of tolerance left an impression on me. I would find them reflecting the Sufi tradition of Islam.

These Irish, English, and Dutch priests were far from home. The church allowed them to return home once in eight years for eight months. They would return to a changing Europe and many would cut short their vacation and hurry home to Pakistan. There was too much change. They mentioned with particular horror the young men called the teddy boys with their sideburns and drainpipes.

Above all, they saw evil incarnate in the young American rock 'n' roll singer, Elvis Presley. Paradoxically, they were finding comfort in a more traditional society – a Muslim society.

My boys' school had a sister boarding school run by nuns for girls, the convent in Murree. This, too, was an elite school and admission was difficult. Benazir Bhutto studied in the convent. Because my wife and sisters studied with the nuns I got to know them over the years. Like the fathers, the mothers impressed me with their humanity. Once again I was left wondering at the scale of their sacrifice.

I did have one complaint against the priests. It haunted me for most of my young years as I learned first hand what injustice feels like. Every time I returned home for the annual winter holidays my parents would bring to my notice the school bill pointing out that I had been breaking windows again at an alarming rate. It was an expensive pastime and my parents were concerned. But I had not broken any windows and I protested vehemently. My friends and I knew that money was being raised to complete the school building. The injustice was really in the response of my parents. They would not hear anything against the priests. Indeed, I would inevitably end up by getting an earful. "How can you even suggest that these good fathers are doing anything wrong?" "Look at the sacrifices they make to educate you." "This time we will overlook your complaining against the fathers."

Pakistan has changed since that time. A bishop killed himself four decades later. He did this in protest at the fate of his community. Persecution and harassment of Christians had become common in Pakistan. The general tolerance in Pakistan society had eroded considerably.

I was not entirely surprised at the attacks on the worshipers in the Pakistani churches after September 11, given the emotions in the region. I just felt a sense of loss. I know that the good decent human beings whom I called fathers, who worked with little or no returns here on earth in difficult times, would have been devastated. But there are also glimmers of hope. Let us turn to a success story in Muslim education.

A success story

In Morocco, most Muslims are confident of their Islam; it is reflected in a new university – Al Akhawayn University (Ahmed 1996). The president, like most of its Muslim staff, is devout, a regular visitor to the mosque. Like his staff, he fasts during the month of Ramadan. He is planning a church and a synagogue on the campus.

The story of the birth of the university is out of the *Arabian Nights*. When offered $50 million as assistance by the King of Saudi Arabia, the King of Morocco, not being able to use the money, wished to return it. The Saudi insisted he keep it. The Moroccan decided to open a world-class university. He called it Al Akhawayn, the two brothers, to reflect the source of funding.

At the physical core of the university is the mosque and adjacent to it an impressive library echoing Islamic tradition. The Greek amphitheater and the American sports complex with its Olympic-sized swimming pool reflect cultural synthesis, as does the fact that this is an English-language university. State-of-the-art communications link its hilltop village of Ifrane to the world. Women account for more than 50 percent of the students. About 30 percent of the faculty is foreign.

I lectured there in 1996 and was grilled on the issue of Islam and women by a young Moroccan woman; the exchange reflected both boldness in the presence of senior faculty and an awareness that was encouraging. The

Moroccan felt that Islam was being misused to deny her certain rights given to her by her religion. It was a charge that echoes throughout the Muslim world. The foreign women were too discreet to touch the subject.

I replied that we needed to look at Islamic civilization as a whole. Islam gave more rights to women than any other religion in the world. Unfortunately some men in Islam denied women those rights or ignorance prevented them from obtaining them. They needed to fight for their legitimate rights.

The significance of an English-language university cannot be overestimated. The Moroccan elite speaks French fluently but the younger generation is turning to English. Some European diplomats were unimpressed with the university, calling it a waste of money, elitist, or a sign of megalomania, like the other brainchild of the king: the new mosque at Casablanca, the largest in Africa.

But for my friend the Pakistani ambassador, who accompanied me, this is one of the great centers of learning in the Muslim world. It proclaims Islam's confidence in its past and vision of the future.

The then Crown Prince of Morocco (now king) in private audience explained the essence of his society to me. Jews, Christians, and Muslims all believe in the same God, he said, and all are essentially the same. This was not just rhetoric. In Morocco the chief adviser to the king on economic affairs is a Jew. There are still 2,000 Jews in Morocco, despite the 100,000–200,000 who migrated to Israel in 1948. A story still circulates of the crown prince's grandfather, who was king during the Second World War. He was asked by Marshal Pétain of France to hand over Morocco's Jews for the Nazi gas chambers (Morocco was a European protectorate). The king refused, saying every single Jew was his responsibility. Neither Muslims nor Jews have forgotten that answer.

Morocco takes pride in its historical links with the tolerant Andalusian civilization that flourished in this region almost a thousand years ago and which linked Spain with North Africa. The contrast in tolerance is sharp with France, where not long ago Muslim schoolgirls were thrown out of school because they wore headscarves. No Europeans have been thrown out of schools in Morocco for *not* wearing such a scarf. Perhaps Morocco has something to teach contemporary Europe.

There are far too few examples of success stories in Muslim education. As a result, Muslim society remains deprived of its own finest traditions. The impact is felt widely and most significantly on Muslim leadership.

4

The Failure of
Muslim Leadership

Ibn Khaldun highlighted the importance of the ruler and his duties to the ruled in this world so that both might aspire to and secure the next. Ibn Khaldun's science of culture ultimately functions to illuminate the science of good governance. In Muslim society the leader embodies both political and moral authority (see Ahmed 1997a, 1997b, 2002a and Najjar 2000). Yet even influential contemporary Western thinkers commenting on Islam, like Huntington and Fukuyama, have failed to discuss the importance of Muslim leadership.

In our time, one of the major crises that faces Muslim society is that of leadership. This crisis affects not only Muslim nations but also their relationship with other countries. Muslim leaders are failing, first, to provide justice (*adl*) and, second, to create the conditions for the existence of compassion and balance (*ihsan*) or knowledge (*ilm*) in their societies.

No self-respecting political or social scientist, reared in the secular or liberal tradition of the West, would dream of looking at the Quran for explanations of political behavior, but that is what we shall do. Muslim social scientists themselves remain in awe of Western social theories and look around for easy answers in Ivy League or Oxbridge or London university departments.

Our thesis is that if the political leadership in its behavior, ideas, and politics is close to the Islamic ideal – as laid out in the Quran and in the life of the Prophet – friction in society is minimal; the further from the Islamic ideal, the greater the tension in society (I first explored this idea in a general sense in Ahmed 2002a; also see 2002b). The primary and greatest model for Muslims is that of the holy Prophet. His life provides the balance between action and spirit, between this world and the next: He is the perfect person, *insan-i-kamil*. Imitating him were those disciples who were closest to him like Umar and Ali, great religious figures. But others too – not seen as religious figures – have attempted to live up to his ideal. Saladin, who retook Jerusalem from the Crusaders in the 12th century, is one such name (his popularity explains why leaders like Saddam Hussein encourage the comparison, especially in times of crisis). The majority of the Muslims see these leaders as exemplary figures. They represent a time when honor was valued.

Ours is not entirely an original route to take. Max Weber persuasively showed us the way in explaining the influence of the Protestant ethic on economic behavior, contra Karl Marx who emphasized economic and material factors as all-important. Inherent in the Weberian model of authority is the assumption that societies move along a secular path, that leadership would be provided by a rational bureaucracy set in a working democracy. However even Weber could not have foreseen the cracking of the civilized veneer and easy reversion to primordial tribalism and savagery in Europe. Germany half a century ago, just a few years after Weber was writing, and the Balkans in the 1990s illustrate for us how fragile is the notion of a staid and safe European civilization based on respect for human life and liberty.

i Muslim Leaders

On the surface, a bewildering range of leadership defies easy categorization: kings, military dictators, mullahs, democrats, and, in the Taliban in Afghanistan, young inexperienced tribal men or religious students (the meaning of Taliban) running large parts of a country. Overshadowing the different kinds of leadership, there are new Muslim movements and a new kind of populist, aggressive, and literalist Muslim leadership that is struggling to emerge. The Taliban and their guest from Saudi Arabia, bin Laden, inspired by men like Sayyid Qutb, perhaps best symbolize this trend. In other Muslim countries, such as Algeria, Egypt, and Pakistan, similar Muslim leaders actively challenge the establishment. Even the Iranians, considered fanatics in the West, complain that the Taliban are so extreme they are giving Islam a bad name.

For these warriors of Islam, the corruption of their rulers, the injustices of their system, and the support some of them enjoy in the West highlight the cultural and political problems that Muslims face, whether in Europe, Africa, or Asia. The seeming indifference of the West to their predicament creates a focus on the West as the enemy.

While the task of the often Westernized post-independent nationalist leaders was to consolidate the state, the task of the new leaders is to destroy it as a legacy of the West and then re-create it in an Islamic mold. The former sought survival in a transitional world; the latter demand purity in an impure one.

Let us construct socio-political categories, however crude, of Muslim leadership. To do so we cut through the confusing conflation, overlap, and collision of several traditions now functioning in the Muslim world: tribal, dynastic, European, and Islamic.

The first of the four categories of Muslim leadership is that of the clerical rulers. Their aim is to restore Islamic faith and practice. They are reacting to the perceived hostility of the world and are therefore inclined to support what I have called hyper-*asabiyya*. Iran is a good example. With the explosive growth of global media from the 1980s onwards, images of this category became the image of the Muslim cleric, indeed of Islam itself: a scowling, evil-looking, bearded figure in black robes, much like the wicked wizard of cartoons.

Iran remains, however much the West is transfixed by it, a one-off example largely explained by its Shia culture and tradition. Whenever given a choice through the polls, Sunni-dominated populations as in Pakistan have rejected the religious parties. The Pakistani Jamaat-i-Islami Party, perhaps the best organized of these religious parties and with the most coherent and sophisticated view of the modern world, has never had more than a few members in parliament. The reason is simple: Islam does not encourage a priesthood. "There is no monkery in Islam," said the Prophet. In normal times the mullah or imam who is hired to lead prayers at the mosque is little more than a lowly paid functionary.

However, in 2002 the traditional electoral pattern was dramatically altered in Pakistan. The people of Pakistan voted for religious parties in large numbers. This is how and why they voted: A vote for the religious parties was a vote against the United States and its man, Musharraf. The Islamophobic statements coming from the United States further enflamed public opinion against the party backed by Musharraf.

The Taliban in Afghanistan are a Sunni exception. The West picked up the word Taliban in the 1990s and incorporated it, like *fatwa* a few years earlier, into the English language. The word comes from *talib* or student in Arabic (Taliban is the plural), but in the Western media it took on the connotation of a violent group of young Muslim fanatics. The Taliban came to power in Afghanistan by default (for more on the Taliban see chapter 6, section i). They were not the historical rulers of the land, neither tribal chiefs nor members of the royal family. With their zeal for Islam and the burning desire to impose their vision on all of society, the Taliban violated two basic tenets of Islam in a manner calculated to cause offense to many in and outside the country: their discrimination against women and the physical beatings that they sometimes administered. Recall the gentleness and kindness of the Prophet of Islam where women were concerned (see next section).

The harshness of the Taliban to minorities, the non-Pukhtun, was also against the spirit of Islam, which encourages tolerance. We need to remember that minorities in Afghanistan were also Muslims. There were far too many cases of non-Pukhtun being not only discriminated against but also treated with violence. This suggests a straightforward ethnic response rather than a religious one, although it may come under the guise of religion. Although ousted from power in Kabul, the Taliban will not disappear. They have returned to their tribal villages and continue to advocate their own brand of Islam. Their inspiration comes from men like Sayyid Qutb.

The Egyptian activist Sayyid Qutb, who was executed by the state in 1966, inspired bin Laden and Al-Qaeda. Qutb was an angry man. He saw around him after the Second World War Muslim society ruled either by corrupt monarchies or by brutal military dictators. Qutb had visited the United States and had come back repelled by its culture, seeing it as the source of global evil. The creation of Israel, which was a defining moment of humiliation and anger for most Arabs, further embittered him. To him, Islam was the only way out of this quagmire. He joined other Muslims who thought like him and were as angry as him. The rules of the brotherhood were clear: hard discipline; secretive communications; complete obedience to the leader and a willingness to make the ultimate sacrifice for the cause.

Qutb set about planning the overthrow of Nasser's government. He was arrested and eventually executed. His death, which is seen as martyrdom by many Muslims, further enhanced his reputation. His extensive writings were so inflammatory that any Egyptian citizen possessing *Milestones*, one of his books, could be arrested and charged with sedition (Qutb n.d.).

Qutb saw modern Western culture as a stereotype, little more than sex, violence, and greed, and rejected it.

> Humanity today is living in a large brothel! One has only to glance at its press, films, fashion shows, beauty contests, ballrooms, wine bars, and broadcasting stations! Or observe its mad lust for naked flesh, provocative postures, and sick, suggestive statements in literature, the arts and the mass media! And add to all this, the system of usury which fuels man's voracity for money and engenders vile methods for its accumulation and investment, in addition to fraud, trickery, and blackmail dressed up in the garb of law. (Armstrong 2000: 240)

Qutb expressed sentiments in his work which can only be described as a generalized and almost irrational prejudice against Jews – in modern parlance anti-Semitism. His preaching has created not only hatred against Jews and therefore Israel, but also of America, which he depicted as being run by Jews.

Qutb's simplistic analysis has had – and still has –

powerful appeal for many ordinary Muslims. The world is divided into *dar al-Islam* (the home of peace or Islam) and *dar al-harb* (the house of war). *Dar al-Islam* can only exist where the state has established the *Shari'a*. The rest of the world is the hostile land of *dar al-harb*. Qutb uses the classical concept of pre-Islamic Arabian society, that of *jahiliya* or ignorance, to describe Muslim leadership. It is the duty of every Muslim to actively overthrow the state of *jahiliya*. He divided Muslim leaders into good and evil, those committed to the rule of God and those opposed to it, the followers of God and the followers of Satan. Qutb's was a starkly black and white view of the world.

The second category of Muslim leaders is that of the military rulers and monarchies (of the former, General Zia in Pakistan used Islam, Saddam did not until the Gulf War; of the latter, the Saudis parade Islam, the Shah of Iran did not). In many countries in this category the already existing tribal structures provided the bare bones of the state structure. Thus the dominant tribal clan of the land simply became the royal rulers, senior administrators, and entrepreneurs after statehood was achieved. Saudi Arabia and the Gulf States are examples. Even the military dictators relied on tribal politics. Both the late Hafez Assad and Saddam Hussein trusted, as far as leaders of this kind can trust, their own sect (in the case of the former) and tribal clan (in the latter).

The third, rather unsuccessful, category is that of the socialist/Communist leader (modeled on Stalin and the Soviet experience), its appeal lying mainly in a rhetoric of care for the poor. Brutal dictators with little hint of Islamic compassion and justice have ruled in this category through the secret police in Iraq and Syria. After the Cold War, this category had little backing or appeal.[1]

The fourth category is the democratic one that includes countries like Egypt, Pakistan, Turkey, and Bangladesh, where elections are held, although there is a history of lapsing into martial law in times of crisis. Stories of corruption, mismanagement, and the collapse of law and order create a general disillusionment with this category.

Leaders in this category skillfully exploit the fears of the West regarding Muslim fundamentalists. Their argument is simple: We are all that stands between you and your worst nightmare, that is, fanatics and Muslim fundamentalists (those in the first category). With the nuclear ambitions of many Muslim countries and the nuclear potential of others, such as Pakistan, this is a genuine concern of the West.

However this style of leadership needs to be developed and strengthened. It reflects the Islamic spirit of egalitarianism, the need for tolerance in plural societies (again reflecting Islam), and larger global trends. Of the four categories, this is the most viable one for our times.

Mohammed Ali Jinnah vs. Osama bin Laden

It is worth looking more closely at one example of a genuine, authentic, and indigenous democratic model. Mohammed Ali Jinnah, the founder of Pakistan, who died in 1948, believed in human rights, women's rights, minority rights, and the rule of the constitution (see Ahmed 1997a, 1997b).

Both supporters and opponents of Jinnah and the Pakistan idea were, paradoxically, expressing their commitment to Islam, but by very different routes. Jinnah would fight for the rights of Muslims through constitutional means; his Muslim critics demanded confrontation and even violence. This opposition has continued to create tension within Muslim society. Bin Laden would symbolize the use of violence to express Muslim discontent just as Jinnah symbolized the use of constitutional means to achieve political ends. Jinnah would succeed in creating the largest Muslim nation on earth in 1947 through a constitutional – not armed – struggle; bin Laden would plunge the world into turmoil in 2001.

Jinnah and bin Laden are at opposite ends of the spectrum. In Britain, Sheikh Umar Bakri's *Khilafah*, the journal of the Hizb-ut-Tahrir, attacked Jinnah as a *kafir*, an insult for a Muslim (December, 1996). Moreover, it accused Jinnah of being an enemy of God and the holy Prophet because Jinnah supported women, Christians, and Hindus and advocated democracy. Why, I asked myself, did they pick on Jinnah? Because, I concluded, Bakri saw him as a major ideological opponent. Significantly, after the American strikes in Sudan and Afghanistan in 1998, Bakri emerged in the media to claim that he represented bin Laden in Europe (also see chapter 5, section i).

In bin Laden and in Jinnah, neatly, we have the two opposing poles of Islam. The former, bearded, in his traditional Muslim clothes, speaking Arabic and of *jihad*; the latter, clean-shaven, in his Savile Row suit, speaking in his English accent and reflecting his Lincoln's Inn education. Which model will prevail in this century?

We know that parents in Pakistan named 10,000 of their newborn sons Osama after 1998 and that bin Laden is a cult figure in much of the Muslim world, with his posters everywhere and even a perfume named after him. I have not come across young men named Jinnah. Certainly no perfume called "Jinnah." What happens in the long term will depend to some extent on Islam's relations with the West. If what is seen as the crusade lasts against Islam the bin Laden model will remain popular among Muslims.

The Taliban leadership may appear "new" to some analysts, and opposed to the ideas of the more Westernized leaders who led the movements after the Second World War, but in fact the division in Muslim leadership goes back to the middle of the 19th century in India. Two distinct models of leadership emerged after the uprisings against the British in 1857: one which came from the newly created college at Aligarh and the other from the newly formed college at Deoband. The two models presented opposed views of the world, although there was a certain degree of overlap in certain areas. Sir Sayyed Ahmed Khan who created the college (later university) at Aligarh on the model of Oxford and Cambridge was a loyal servant of the British Raj and wished to synthesize Islam with modernity (Ahmed 1997a). The founder of Deoband fought the British in a *jihad* during the uprisings and his influential college created networks throughout India, which have over time influenced groups like the Taliban. The schism in Muslim leadership is thus rooted in the indigenous response to modernity and the threatening presence of Western imperialism.

In any case we must be cautious with our categories. Pakistan illustrates that one country can reflect various categories: Under Jinnah it was democratic; under Ayub, a military dictatorship; under Zia, an Islamic dictatorship; and under Musharraf, it has returned to a straightforward military dictatorship attempting to manipulate the electoral process. Under the Bhuttos, father and daughter, and Nawaz Sharif it was a democracy but a somewhat ramshackle one. Each category will confront problems in the future unless the core features of society we have identified are repaired.

ii   Veiled Truth: Women in Islam

The terrible events of September 11 opened a Pandora's box of questions about Islam, including: Does Islam treat women as second-class citizens? When *asabiyya* is functioning in normal times women have an important and integral role to play in society. They are also protected by an understood code of behavior. In times of change and disruption men practice hyper-*asabiyya*, which invariably targets the women of other opposed groups. To dishonor the women of the enemy is to dishonor the enemy.

Questions about women have become a staple for media discussion. Too often, the answers people devise are an excuse to express their inherent prejudice and even ignorance. The challenge for Muslims is to throw light on these questions with two distinct audiences in mind: the Western media, which tends to reflect its own prejudices about Islam; and Muslims who see the answers to such questions through the prism of a distorted anger and hatred of the world around them.

Women in Islam are central to domestic and cultural life, and their role is a critical one in society. Groups such as the Taliban, as is by now well known, have a poor way of showing their appreciation for women. They ban women from holding jobs outside the home and even from being seen in public places. This drives an already suppressed section of the population into further subjugation, as many women – in Afghanistan, for instance – have to fend for their families after having lost their husbands in the civil wars. Women, therefore, must carry a double burden.

I believe that there is a clear correlation between the treatment of women and Muslim self-perception, which bears upon the position of women in Islam (Ahmed 2002a). When Muslim society is confident and in a state of balance, it treats women with fairness and respect. When Muslim society is threatened and feels vulnerable, it treats women with indifference and even harshness.

This simple correlation can be tested against history. During the early days of Islam, women played a distinct and full role in society. Indeed, their position was pre-eminent. It is no coincidence that, when asked, "Which is the short-cut to paradise?" the Prophet of Islam replied, "Under the feet of the mother," meaning that the path to paradise lies at the feet of the mother; that is, the mother is so highly elevated in society that her offspring must care for her and respect her.

Indeed, in Muslim history the privilege of being the first Muslim goes to Khadijah, the Prophet's wife. She was older and wealthier than him and from an aristocratic background. Previously widowed, Khadijah initiated the marriage proposal, too. She remained the ideal wife, consoling the Prophet in loss, encouraging him in his great mission, and never doubting him when he announced his message to the world. He was inconsolable when she died. Their daughter Fatimah also played a key role in Islamic history. Fatimah was the wife of Ali and the mother of Hassan and Hussein from whom are descended the Sayyeds, the holiest lineage in Muslim society. The family of Fatimah is particularly revered in Shia tradition, which is strong in Iran.

Even in this phase of Islamic history, women led armies (Aishah), were famous as Sufi saints (Rabia), and were rulers in their own right (Razia of India). They wielded immense power both privately and publicly. Their names have been conferred on towns (Madinah al-Zahra in Andalusia) and coins of the realm (the Mughal empress Noor Jahan).

Even if this is a somewhat idealized picture of Islamic women, the sad comparison with their present situation raises many questions. It is almost as if a catastrophe took place to alter their status so dramatically. I believe the reason for the drastic change in Islamic women's status lies in the 19th and 20th centuries, when European powers colonized Muslim lands. This period of colonization affected society both internally and externally. There was a loss of confidence, which resulted in a loss of tolerance. Muslim men reacted to this loss, not unnaturally, by doing what they thought was necessary for the protection and integrity of their families. They secluded their women from the prying eyes of foreign troops. Burkhas, the black, tent-like attire women wear, became common. Women were restricted to the home.

This image provided fodder for Orientalist scholars to depict Muslim women, especially in the harem, as characteristic of the decadence of Islam itself. It was a time of retreat and confusion. When the Europeans left in the middle of the 20th century, Muslim women once again emerged in public in varying degrees, but they were left to fight now-entrenched local traditions and male views and prejudices. Some of these have virtually nothing to do with Islam. For example, unmarried or widowed women do not inherit property in some parts of the Muslim world. Their male relatives make excuses and pass off their greed as Islamic law. A woman demanding rights or insisting on her own career could be in trouble. There is an old proverb in Pakistan and Afghanistan: "For a woman, either the *kor* (house) or the *gor* (grave)." In traditional homes, the main role of the wife has become to serve her husband. This is reflected in another proverb: "Husband is another name for god."

Polygamy itself has become a distorted practice. In Islam, a man can take another wife only under certain circumstances. The Quran made provision for a man to "marry as many women as you wish, two or three or four"

(Surah 4: Verse 3). This made sense at a time of war, when there were many widowed women and sometimes they fell on hard times. It was also a sociological mechanism to ensure that men with barren wives could marry again and reproduce. It was certainly not a license for lust, as suggested by Orientalist fantasies of the harem. The Quran clearly states, and many religious scholars have argued, that polygamy itself may not be feasible. This is because the Quran insists that if a man marries more than one wife, he must treat the wives exactly alike: "If you fear not to treat them equally, marry only one," it warns, "Indeed, you will not be able to be just between your wives, even if you try" (ibid).

In past decades, as Muslim society has attempted to come to grips with the forces of modernity, a range of remarkable women has emerged to challenge prejudice and provide direction. South Asia, where I come from, has produced a number of outstanding female leaders. Fatimah Jinnah played a central role in aiding her brother M. A. Jinnah who led the movement for Pakistan, becoming a role model for South Asian women. She gave up a potentially successful career as a dentist to stand shoulder to shoulder with her brother in the colossal battle for Pakistan in the 1940s.

After her brother's death, when General Ayub Khan declared martial law in Pakistan, Fatimah Jinnah became the symbol of opposition to military dictatorship. A generation later, Benazir Bhutto challenged another military dictator and became the first female Muslim prime minister anyplace. Bangladesh, too, has had several female prime ministers. In 2001 Megawati Sukarnoputri became the president of Indonesia, the largest Muslim nation in the world. There are now distinguished female ambassadors and members of parliament in many countries throughout the Muslim world.

The majority of ordinary Muslim women, however, are still trapped in local, tribal codes and customs that do not permit them to benefit from their Islamic heritage. Islam itself remains only half understood. The recovery from the colonial past has been too slow and painful, the sense of the future uncertain. Until Muslim scholars and intellectuals are able to come to terms with history, they will not be able to repair the damage. The success of a few outstanding women will do little to improve the lot of the majority of Muslim women. Only with widespread education and the restoration of Muslim confidence can contemporary Muslim women assume their rightful place in society: It is only then that the Prophet's saying about paradise lying at the feet of the mother will have meaning.

Gender and honor

During times of conflict, especially between different religious civilizations, women become both the symbol of honor and the target to be dishonored. The following is an account of how women take on this role between civilizations at war. It records the ideas of an Arab during the crusades in the 12th century:

> To the Arab scribe Imad ad-Din, the wailing of the women was amusing, for he regarded all European women as licentious whores, glowing with ardor for carnal intercourse. The mere thought of them sent him into rapturous flights of medieval pornography. European women were "proud and scornful, foul-fleshed and sinful, ardent and inflamed, tinted and painted, desirable and appetising, exquisite and graceful, seductive and languid, desired and desiring, pink-faced and unblushing, black-eyed and bullying, with shapely buttocks and nasal voices, broken-down little fools. . . . They dedicated as a holy offering what they kept between their thighs". (Reston 2002: 93–4)

Almost a millennium later little seems to have changed with regards to gender and honor when different civilizations clash. When the talk is of honor women become symbols of honor. To humiliate women is to humiliate the enemy. Recently women have been singled out as special targets. It is the cruel, perverted interpretation of honor in our time. Arundhati Roy describes the link between gender and religious violence (in "Democracy: Who's She When She's at Home?" in *Outlook India*, magazine, May 6, 2002):

> Last night a friend from Baroda [in India] called. Weeping. It took her fifteen minutes to tell me what the matter was. It wasn't very complicated. Only that Sayeeda, a friend of hers, had been caught by a mob. Only that her stomach had been ripped open and stuffed with burning rags. Only that after she died, someone carved 'OM' [Hindu invocation of the divine] on her forehead. Precisely which Hindu scripture preaches this?

Rape as policy

Rape and its frequent use in our time is a symptom of hyper-*asabiyya*. It is one of the most infamous acts on man's long list of infamy, one suggesting deep emotional disturbance and cultural prejudice. Because rape is so intimately tied to ideas of dishonor and disgrace people are reluctant to discuss it. Yet to learn about the true nature of ethnic and religious conflict social scientists must study rape and sexual intimidation in the context of that society.

We know that in Bosnia rape was used deliberately as an instrument of war (Ahmed 1993b). Dogs, men who carry the HIV virus, and gangs taking turns were used in the rape camps. Soldiers gang-raped small girls in front of their mothers. Civilians, administrators, students – ordinary people – were all involved as active participants or as spectators in the Bosnian rape camps. They cheered on their compatriots.

More recently, there is considerable evidence gathered by international human rights organizations and by Indian writers that Indian troops in Kashmir have been using the same tactics. And after the destruction of the Ayodhya mosque, the police were clearly implicated in organizing riots in Bombay and Surat against Muslims that involved rape. Iraq and Israel (the former in a crude way, the latter in a more subtle manner) have also used sexual tactics to intimidate minorities. According to the Iraqi expatriate author of *Cruelty and Silence* Iraqi soldiers force Kurdish women from camps and take them to be raped (Makiya 1993); Israelis lock up Arab women in security cells for the night with threatening men. An organization of courageous Israeli women risked the wrath of the authorities by documenting such cases in *Women for Women Political Prisoners*, published in Jerusalem in December 1989.

The woman is twice punished: by the brutality of the act and by the horror of her family. Notions of modesty and motherhood are violated. Rape strikes families at their most vulnerable point, especially in traditional societies where, in certain tribes, illegitimate sexual acts are punished by death (Ahmed 1980, 1991). Rape is thus deliberately employed by ethnic neighbors who are fully aware of its expression as political power and cultural assertion to humiliate the internal other.

The use of religion to motivate soldiers on the battlefield is not new. What is unexpected in a time that so self-consciously regards itself as "modern" is the invocation of the divine to justify violent acts like rape. Throughout history, soldiers have committed rape but religion has never endorsed such behavior. But today rape is being used in an almost calculated manner by troops representing the majority, often backed by parts of the state structure, and linked in a perverse way to an idea of the divine. The rapists hope to dishonor the enemy by raping their women. But the society of the victim will say the rapists have no honor.

Muslim youths in Indonesia yell *"Allah-ho-Akbar"* – (God is great) – while assaulting Chinese women. Christians and Hindus in the Balkans and India respectively have invoked the divine while raping Muslims. Quite apart from the brutality aimed at the women themselves, such acts of violence are not only meant as straightforward cultural humiliation but express something more sinister and complex.

What is the perverse logic that connects the divine to these acts of savagery? The divine is being used here to hurt and humiliate. This is a double failure: the failure of the rapists in their common humanity and the failure of the traditional interpreters of the divine to communicate ideas of compassion and piety.

The sociological implications of this manner of rape are clear: Rape as a final line divides one group from the other; the state, through its male troops, becomes the rapist, raping its own citizens, those it is sworn to protect. Bitterness is at a peak. So is the nature of hatred in the response. Blood and revenge follow. A spiral of violence is set in motion. All the key notions of modernity – justice, rule of law, rationalism, and civic society – are negated by the criminal nature of ethnic rape. For the victim and her family it is no longer an age of modernity and progress but one of barbarism and darkness.

5

Searching for a Muslim Ideal: Inclusion

Muslims, wherever they live, are aware of the crisis in their societies, if not of the Khaldunian explanation of its breakdown. They react according to their ideas and capabilities. We have identified two broadly opposed responses in the midst of many, and we will discuss them as they affect other civilizations: one is to advocate a policy of inclusion, in the hope of generating dialogue and understanding; the other, to encourage activities promoting exclusion, confrontation, and rejection. The former wish for dialogue and harmony; they are aware of a greater common humanity. For them human destiny is shared and the coming time is one that could bring different societies and peoples together. They draw their inspiration from their faith. Those who take the opposed position, those who believe in exclusion, also draw their inspiration from their faith. However they interpret their faith in a literalist and narrow manner; those who are not like them are beyond the pale. They are prepared to reject – often with violence – those who do not share their way of thinking. Their wrath, however, is not confined to those of other faiths; it is aimed also at members of their own community who think differently.

Below I will discuss two extended case studies based on differing Muslim approaches to the world. The first is autobiographical. I will share some personal matters, as this method will allow us to view Muslim society comprehensively. The second case examines the approach of the Taliban, who in some senses are good representatives of the idea and practice of exclusion.

i   Case Study One: The Scholarship of Inclusion

Over a decade before September 11, 2001, which forced the world to raise some central questions about Islam – is Islam a religion of violence? Is Islam compatible with democracy? Is there genuine democratic leadership in the Islamic world? – I had set out to explore these very questions. In doing so I hoped to force a debate within Muslim society and was therefore prepared to confront the controversy which was bound to follow. The scale and intensity of the reaction unleashed forces that almost destroyed me.

Attempting the scholarship of inclusion

The controversy around *The Satanic Verses* was about to explode when I arrived in Cambridge University in late 1988 to take up the Iqbal Fellowship.[1] I was pushed into the debate about Islam among scholars, in the community, and in the media. I discussed Islam with many people including young Muslims whom the media depicted as angry young men with hatred in their eyes and the word "kill" on their lips. The hijackers of September 11 would be like them, indeed then about the same age and of a similar background. I set myself the task of challenging the sense of anger and hatred in the Muslim world. I believed it diminished the capacity to discover the glory and compassion of God in heaven and encouraged imbalance and insecurity here on earth.

From the vantage point of Cambridge University, I set myself the ambitious task of recording and attempting to repair the Khaldunian breakdown. I spent more than a decade writing scholarly books on the subject, making media appearances and films about it and organizing people to help me repair it. Projects such as the six-part BBC television series *Living Islam*[2] and the Jinnah Quartet were initiated and completed. Seen as landmark events, these projects helped to change the negative climate around Islam, and they assisted in the start of serious interfaith dialogue.

The Jinnah Quartet, based on the life of M. A. Jinnah, the founder of Pakistan, took me a decade to complete. It included a feature film, *Jinnah*; a documentary, *Mr. Jinnah: The Making of Pakistan*; an academic book, *Jinnah, Pakistan and Islamic Identity: The Search for Saladin* (Ahmed 1997a); and a graphic novel, *The Quaid: Jinnah and the Story of Pakistan* (Ahmed 1997b). The Quartet attempted to answer the question: Do Muslims have leaders who care for human rights, women's rights, minority rights, and the sanctity of the constitution and who can lead their nations to the community of world civilizations? I believed Jinnah was one such leader who had provided a relevant model.

It is well to keep in mind that what most people knew of Jinnah would derive from his negative portrayal in Richard Attenborough's film *Gandhi* or books like *Freedom at Midnight* (Collins and Lapierre 1994; originally published in 1976). The Jinnah Quartet was challenging established images and ideas of the last days of the British Raj.

The projects took me all over the world to meet scholars, potential investors, and those interested in the subject.

At one level Muslim royalty rallied: the Crown Prince – now King – of Morocco; the Crown Prince of Jordan; a prince from the house of Saud in Saudi Arabia. So did ordinary Muslims, sometimes with just their affectionate support and prayers. Muslim society opened before me in all its forms and shapes and I noted its moods, behavior, practices, and thinking.

Great debate, controversy, and passion were aroused by the projects. This was understandable: they were not just changing images in the media, in itself a major challenge, but touching on central issues in society such as leadership, the nature of the state, and the status of women and minorities. Above all, they emphasized the compassionate and tolerant nature of Islam. Religious, ethnic, and national boundaries were being crossed and people were as ready to dismiss and debunk as they were to support.

The scars of battle

But defending such positions comes at a cost. Hurdles were put in the path of these projects, even from inside. For instance, during the shooting of the film *Jinnah* in 1997 the Pakistani media, led by an editor who had failed to get the role of Jinnah, alleged that Salman Rushdie had written the script for the film.[3]

The lie was highly irresponsible, as in Pakistan the name of Rushdie is considered almost in the same light as that of the devil himself. Ayatollah Khomeini issued the *fatwa* against the author after being told that Pakistanis had been shot to death while protesting at *The Satanic Verses*. The rumor about Rushdie persisted even when he denied it in a letter to the *Guardian* (May 7, 1997) and was only laid to rest when he refuted it on the BBC radio show "Start the Week" hosted by Melvyn Bragg on June 16, 1997. But the show on which we appeared together generated another round of accusations against me by some Muslims. I was taken to task for being a lax Muslim because I failed to implement the *fatwa* by not leaping across the studio table and doing Rushdie in.

Some critics saw these endeavors as part of a Zionist conspiracy, others as a Hindu one.[4] The former suspicion was no doubt confirmed in some minds in 1999 when I became the first Muslim to be invited by the Liberal and Progressive Synagogues of the UK to deliver the annual Rabbi Goldstein Memorial Lecture in the central synagogue in St John's Wood, London.

Earlier I had been invited to talk at evensong in Selwyn College Chapel, Cambridge, and was the first Muslim don to be given that honor. The events were widely covered in the British media and seen as significant steps in interfaith dialogue. While most Muslims supported the initiatives, some were unhappy. A few argued that Jews and Christians were "enemies" and that to visit their places of worship was akin to blasphemy for a Muslim. Sheikh Umar Bakri's supporters attacked me in the press. I was walking perilously close to *fatwa* territory.

Patterns of post-honor behavior

Jinnah was jinxed, I had been warned when I began the project. An American professor had died while writing an earlier script for a different project, and a documentary version had been shelved. In my case *Jinnah* appeared jinxed too – there was resignation from service, dislocation from the UK, irrational attempts to sabotage the project, and financial and family hardship. In spite of the enormous support across the country, including that of high-profile figures like Farooq Leghari, the former president of Pakistan, and Benazir Bhutto, the former prime minister, there appeared to be a pall over the project.

Believing that they reduced the Jinnah film to farce I had two Stygian characters, a ghostly boatman and a *djinn*, edited out. Robert Ashby (born Rashid Suhrawardy), who played Nehru in the film, quipped that we were battling to salvage *Jinnah* from *Djinnah*. The answers however, I am suggesting, are not in mystical explanations, the evil eye, or mumbo jumbo, but in sociology. This is the dark side of Muslim society.

Looking at the breakdown of society for a Muslim scholar is like staring into the face of despair.[5] There were those whom I had brought onto the project who were far from exemplary in their behavior: In the refusal to give accounts; in ignoring the queries about irregularities; in cold-bloodedly plotting to take over the project; in deliberately launching a smear campaign based on lies and innuendos to divert attention; and in exaggerating their own role in the production – I was witnessing the collapse of honorable behavior in the Westernized Muslim elite.

In order to understand this puzzle let us turn to an anthropologist who has worked in Muslim society. Charles Lindholm conducted fieldwork in north Pakistan and wrote up his work under the title *Generosity and Jealousy* (1982). Society, he argued, was motivated primarily by ideas of generosity and jealousy. This is not an entirely new insight (we have already heard Yusuf Ali's comments on Muslim jealousy in chapter 3, section ii).

However it points to something important in the context of our discussion. Because *asabiyya* has broken down and there is little or no honor, individual behavior is influenced by personal and emotional reasons. During the decade I worked on the Jinnah project, I encountered generosity but also obsessive jealousy. This erratic oscillation from one point to the other was a challenge to Islam itself, which by definition, essentially and ultimately, must create a social order based on balance. Except for some honorable exceptions I saw little justice, compassion, or knowledge in the behavior of individuals who were supposed to be leaders in society. Indeed I saw many who appeared to have little idea of honor; they were citizens of a post-honor world.

My failure perhaps was not to heed Christopher Lee, the star of *Jinnah*. "Stop being a professor. Don't be so trusting. Be a producer. You are dealing with sharks and they will eat you up," Lee had consistently warned me. Lee was extremely dissatisfied with the director of the film and expressed his unhappiness wherever he could (in the revised version of his autobiography he acknowledges the key people associated with the film, except the director – see Epilogue, *Jinnah*, in Lee 1997).

When I was appointed the Pakistan high commissioner in London in October 1999, I joined with enthusiasm, hoping to bring change. But I encountered more problems than jealousy and malice. I was warned by Pakistani intelligence services in London not to talk so much of Jinnah and compassionate Islam and to concentrate on projecting the regime in Islamabad.

Other initiatives were killed. For example, I called on the Archbishop of Canterbury at Lambeth Palace with eminent Pakistani Christians, including Bishop Michael Nazir Ali. The archbishop normally does not receive high commissioners or ambassadors but knew my work in interfaith dialogue. I invited the archbishop to Pakistan to encourage interfaith dialogue in that country. I knew the minorities in Pakistan felt persecuted and this visit would help create good will. However some senior figures in Islamabad registered their unhappiness and sabotaged the visit. The mullahs would be unhappy, they argued. This was when the Taliban were still the protégés of the rulers of Islamabad: Senior people in government called them "my boys." Later, my invitation to the archbishop would be used as a black mark against me.

I was appalled at the narrow-mindedness and embarrassed because the archbishop had accepted the invitation in good faith while aware of the potential difficulties it posed. I had discussed the invitation with General Pervez Musharraf and he had been excited and urged me to hasten the visit. He was seen then as a pariah in the international community and this visit would help him. After assuring me of full support he backed down under pressure from the Pakistan Foreign Office, performing the kind of flip-flop that would later characterize him on the global stage.

The Indians from the time of my appointment had singled me out as someone who could make a difference on the international stage on behalf of Pakistan (see, for example, *India Today*, December 6, 1999). Now seeing an opportunity to dislodge a Pakistan high commissioner, they launched a media campaign based on slander and innuendo through the director of my *Jinnah* film.[6]

Musharraf, after assuming power, was soon surrounded by sycophants convincing him of his divine destiny, and he began exhibiting tendencies toward megalomania. One of the courtiers, a Pakistani American from Washington DC, proclaimed loudly and repeatedly after September 11 that Musharraf was once a "pariah" but now he was a "messiah": Musharraf, obviously possessing an ear for rhythm, promptly made him a minister.[7]

Musharraf had assured me of his full support in personal correspondence – "I assure you of my full support for the dedicated hard work that you are putting in . . . You will always have my backing" – yet within weeks he had succumbed to the intrigues of the Pakistan Foreign Office, withdrawn his "backing," and agreed to transfer me. No reasons were given. I wrote to Musharraf demanding an inquiry and if I was found innocent of the nonsense in the press fueled by the Pakistan Foreign Office, a public apology. If this was happening to a high commissioner, I pointed out, what hope was there of an ordinary Pakistani receiving justice? I received no reply.

In the end, feeling betrayed by my own team, I resigned in disgust.[8] It was the only honorable course of action left, I wrote in my resignation letter. I had joined a different service in a different Pakistan in 1966 when I was appointed to the elite Civil Service of Pakistan on the basis of the competitive exams for the Central Superior Services. I had held key appointments in the field with distinction and had been given many commendations and awards including the Star of Excellence. I had made many friends and admirers. Now I found that as the word of my resignation spread some of them abandoned me. When I arrived in the United States shortly afterward and inquired about the back pay and pensions that the government owed me, even the Pakistan ambassador in Washington, whom I had known for two decades, was too busy to return my calls. A nonsensical smear campaign in the Pakistan press, which bore the hallmark of official agencies, questioned my patriotism on the basis of the Indian star in *Jinnah*. My brother, a brigadier in the army, received visits by sullen colleagues who let him know of the dire consequences if I criticized Musharraf.

I believe several forces came together, directly or indirectly, forming unlikely allies to sabotage the projection of the ideas of Jinnah through the Jinnah Quartet. The Quartet had become a powerful vehicle of ideas and therefore a catalyst for change. My orders recalling me to

Islamabad were issued in early June 2000, the day after *Jinnah* was released in Urdu and English in Pakistan. Was I being punished for making *Jinnah*?

"Honor comes from God"

During those difficult years, what kept me going was my faith in the Quranic verse which says that *izzat* (honor) and *zillat* (dishonor) are from God alone. They are not from the military or civil dictators in Islamabad. Nor from society. As an anthropologist I understood this to mean that society ensures justice and sooner or later truth prevails. Equally important was the love and support of my wife, my children, my family, and my friends.

My difficulties reminded me of Muslim history going back to the earliest time in South Asia. The first warrior to make a name for and in South Asian Islam was the young commander Muhammad bin Qasim. He landed on the coast near what is now Karachi and conquered what is now the Pakistan province of Sind for Islam in the early years of the 8th century. He was defamed by his enemies and without a proper trial he was stitched into a leather bag and sent back to Baghdad, the seat of the Islamic kingdom. He suffocated to death. The tragedy was not only the death itself; the tragedy was the manner and cause of his punishment. It was not the accusation of sexual harassment by the Indian princesses, which they later recanted, but the arbitrary manner of the punishment. It appears no one bothered to ask whether he was guilty or not. No one bothered to relate the reasons for the complaint to his achievements and therefore establish the cause of the complaint.

Although there were no princesses involved – Indian or otherwise – the accusations against me were analogous. I was accused of being every kind of agent – Hindu, Zionist,

Islamic – and condemned in the press without trial. If they had their way I felt my critics would have had me stitched up in a leather bag. The reason, I felt, was primarily malice and jealousy. This side of Muslim justice and this aspect of Muslim nature, it appeared, had not changed.

Was it worth it?

Some not so influenced by notions of idealism, and more interested in keeping ledgers, may well ask: Was it worth it? They will point to the physical dangers, the lies and slander, the financial sacrifices, and the emotional exhaustion. My answer may be different from that of those who love me – especially the women in my life, my mother, my daughters, and my wife, who stood with me, shoulder to shoulder, and without whom the projects I have alluded to here would have been unmanageable, if not impossible. They were concerned that I had taken on a global challenge unnecessarily and was being exposed to personal danger in a turbulent society and time. The answer therefore is difficult and complex.

These projects and their theme of dialogue and understanding were not only changing British royalty[9] and creating understanding for Islam[10] but were also having an effect on ordinary Muslims.[11] Religious leaders of all shades responded to my work – some positively, [12] others not. Sheikh Umar Bakri, whom we saw in the last chapter attacking Jinnah and declaring himself the chief representative of bin Laden in Europe, disliked intensely my attempts at interfaith dialogue in the UK. Bakri attacked me in Adam Lebor's book, *A Heart Turned East: Among the Muslims of Europe and America* (1997). Bakri called me a "chocolate Muslim" and "an Uncle Tom" because "he [Akbar Ahmed] admires Western civilization more than

Islamic civilization . . . He is a sincere Muslim but sincere is not enough." (ibid: 142–5). In October 2001, Bakri was in the news again. He had sent his followers to Afghanistan to fight against the Americans and the British; British ministers declared this was treason.

Most important, the young were being influenced by the Jinnah project. After a seminar at Princeton University in March 2001, a student introduced himself to me as a Pakistani from Lahore. He said he had an eight-year-old nephew who would tell him that he wished to grow up to join the Pakistan army in order to kill Hindus. But after seeing the *Jinnah* film, he said he wanted to grow up to be another Jinnah, and a man of justice and peace. The change in the world-view of the little boy in Lahore would justify the sacrifices and the tribulations in the battle for ideas; he owns this century.

When the various projects were completed I was humbled to know that the road was littered with aborted projects of a similar nature and the cemetery full of scholars less intellectually and culturally ambitious than we were. Take the example of *Atatürk*, the proposed film project about the founder of modern Turkey, which was abandoned due to the opposition to it about the time we were battling for *Jinnah*. Antonio Banderas, who was to play Atatürk, received so many death threats that he backed out.

It had been a long and tiring decade for me. I had helped to change the image of Islam and had taken initiatives in interfaith dialogue. But I had changed too. I was exhausted and needed to withdraw from the world for a while. In the summer of 2000 I severed my links with the bureaucracy of Pakistan and headed for Princeton University.

The rhythm of campus life, the enthusiasm of my students, the affection and generosity of my host and friend Professor Lawrence Rosen, and the excitement of being at one of the finest universities in the world helped to revivify my spirit. The discussions on campus encouraged me to consider the previous decade and to extract theoretical and intellectual conclusions from my experiences.

I have given the reader a personal glimpse of what it is like to engage in the current debate about civilizations and the price that may come with it. The reader may also, perhaps, appreciate why the life of Ibn Khaldun has a resonance for me.

ii Inclusivists in America: Islam in Toledo, Ohio

A historian coming upon the Islamic Center of Greater Toledo, Ohio, would be forgiven for doing a double take. The picture-postcard Islamic Center with its dome and soaring minarets could be from Toledo, Spain, a thousand years ago; the background adds to the impression – the open vistas, the neat green fields, and the deep far sky. Perhaps I was over-anxious to locate the New Andalusia (see chapter 1, section ii).

So confident and striking is the Islamic Center that it has become a symbol of Islam in Ohio. Toledo views the Center with pride. It features in the city's local brochures and publicity material.

That is why when, after September 11, some unknown and angry people shot bullets at the Center, the Christian community rallied. Local radio stations announced a public show of support. Large numbers turned up at the Center and formed human rings around it, ready to defend it. The Christian response reassured and calmed the Muslim community.

In Washington, I had heard much about Toledo's Muslim community. So when the Islamic Center and the University of Toledo invited me early in May, 2002, I was curious to discover how they have achieved such tolerance and integration.

Ohio is a long way from the hothouse atmosphere in Washington DC, which is so media – and policy – driven. Ohio appears more in touch with itself; more a part of "real" America. This is the Midwest of America, the heartland.

I noted three distinct and unusual features regarding gender at the Islamic Center. First, it had voted for the first female president of a Muslim center in America (while I was there the news broke that she had been appointed as a judge by the State – perhaps another first). Secondly, there was no rigid dress code for women as long as they were modestly dressed, and while some wore the *hijab*, others did not. Thirdly, the main prayer is conducted with women and men praying together separated by a three-foot partition that runs through the center of the hall. The women therefore do not pray behind the men but alongside them.

The Islamic Center, clean and well run, had a friendly atmosphere. Muslims and non-Muslims mingled freely, and there was none of the tension that sometimes marks Islamic centers. In particular, I found the women to be active and assertive.

My host, Dr Amjad Hussain, a prominent surgeon, kept me busy for the three days I was there with lectures, speeches, and community functions. I met young and old, women and men, Muslim and non-Muslim. At the Zohr prayer on Sunday, I was invited to speak to the congregation of about 400. I spoke of the importance of knowledge and tolerance. I gave the example of Muslim Spain when Jews, Christians, and Muslims lived together harmoniously and created a rich civilization. The previous evening I had shown Part II of *Living Islam*, called "The Challenge of the Past," and suggested that the great days of Islam were the great days of knowledge and tolerance. I noted with interest the cultural synthesis behind the podium from where I spoke: the flag of the United States, the Stars and Stripes, alongside a picture of the grand mosque in Mecca.

The question and answer sessions brought out some interesting trends in Toledo. The Islamic Center may be a strong model but it is only one model. There are four other mosques in the city. There are two African-American mosques, one of them run by the Nation of Islam; there is a Shia mosque; and there is a big central mosque in town, which has an approach distinct from that of the Islamic Center. Still, there was enough general good will for the imam of the city's central mosque to come to hear my lectures and invite me to talk to the annual function his mosque was planning in the fall.

Why, I asked myself, was the Islamic Center different? I believe the answer rests largely in the leadership. The central leadership is educated (university professors and senior professionals), affluent, and determined to create an enlightened and tolerant Islamic vision for the community. Its ethnic background helps reinforce its vision. Lebanese, Palestinians, Syrians – the spillover from Detroit, which has the largest concentration of Arabs in the United States – and South Asians work together with ease.

Take the example of my friend Dr Amjad Hussain. Born in Peshawar in the North-West Frontier Province of Pakistan, he came to Toledo more than three decades ago as a young doctor. He married Dottie, a warm and supportive American woman, and has lived happily with his family in Toledo ever since. Dottie and Amjad are respected members of the community and have been important in shaping the Islamic Center.

While Dr Amjad is a devout Muslim, he is also a tolerant one with a sense of humor. His wife remains a Christian. Indeed, when a Pakistani reporter asked him with a certain tension in his voice: "I hope you have converted your wife to Islam?" Dr Amjad replied: "No, but I have become a Christian."

The Hussain home, where they hosted a large dinner for me, is a good example of interfaith and intercultural goodwill. They have friends from every section of society. But Dr Amjad's heart remains in the North-West Frontier Province. His car bears the number plate "NWFP 1".

Still, there was an underlying concern, which soon manifested itself in my conversations with the community. Many of the young generation are angry and disenchanted after September. They have fallen back to isolation. This trend concerns the leaders of the Islamic Center.

If Dr Amjad, his colleagues at the Islamic Center and others like them succeed in the coming time, then Muslims will be able both to contribute to and integrate in society with their dignity and honor intact. If not, there will be conflict.

I have illustrated the route inclusivists are taking to respond to the Khaldunian breakdown. Other Muslims have taken different routes, their endeavors also raising controversy and debate. One such group is the Taliban who are criticized by many, and not only in the West, for their treatment of women and the minorities. They remain a mystery to the world and it is to them that we now turn.

6

Searching for a Muslim Ideal: Exclusion

Because so little is known of the Taliban in Afghanistan, now seemingly on the wane, several false assumptions are made about them: that they are simply a political party; that they are defined and contained by Afghanistan; that they are a passing phenomenon and quite marginal to the Muslim world; and that by ignoring them or bombing them they will fade into oblivion. I am suggesting that the Taliban who had set out to reinforce disintegrating *asabiyya* locally had ended up creating a state driven by hyper-*asabiyya*.

The books and articles on the Taliban simply confirm the negative media images of Islam by pegging their ideas to clichés such as "terrorist Islam," "*jihad*," and "fundamentalist." Take Rashid's title, *Taliban: Militant Islam, Oil and Fundamentalism in Central Asia* (2000), Stern's sub-headings: "Schools of Hate," "Jihad International Inc," "Addicted to Jihad," "Bad Boys," and "Exporting Holy War" (2000), or Vollmann's stereotypical Taliban (2000). The problem of representation is compounded for the Taliban, as they appear to be practicing the scholarship of exclusion. We are left with few insights into what is happening and why in their society.[1]

After September 2001 Americans saw the Taliban as the enemy supporting Al-Qaeda and bin Laden. In the process they dismissed Afghanistan as a backward tribal society. While America until half a century ago was dominated by the descendants of white, Northern European Protestants and there was open prejudice and often violence against minorities, Afghanistan was then a much more tolerant society than it would become half a century later. The king, who was ousted in 1973, believed that his duty was to ensure that all his subjects, irrespective of their religious or tribal background, were given their rights and his protection. Indeed Afghanistan was a haven for young Americans looking to free themselves from the strictures of Western life. Drugs and sex were not the only attractions in the 1960s to those on the hippie trail to India that led through Kabul. Afghanistan was also a stable, culturally rich, and scenic land.

The collapse of the monarchy, the Soviet invasion, the long, bitter struggle against the occupying forces, and the civil war that followed the withdrawal of the Soviets resulted in the collapse of the traditional structures. Tribal chiefs and elders were in disarray. In the political vacuum strong tribal leaders, warlords, disregarding traditional boundaries and codes of behavior, roamed the land.

Afghans were exhausted with the state of civil war in the land in the early 1990s. They were desperate for stability and integrity in the administration. They saw the fusion of Pukhtun custom and Islamic tradition that the Taliban represented as a possible direction for the future. Many of the Taliban had been educated in Pakistan. A narcissistic relationship existed between the Pukhtuns on either side of the international border, which almost made the border itself irrelevant. Poppy cultivation was strictly banned, law and order enforced, and bribery and corruption in the administration were controlled. The Taliban way appeared to work for a short while in the Pukhtun areas of Afghanistan along the eastern border with Pakistan.

The Taliban, however, were the victims of their success. Once they moved out of the Pukhtun areas and occupied most of Afghanistan, including Kabul, their simple vision of the world no longer worked. It was not acceptable to those tribes who were not Pukhtun. Besides, the urbanized Afghans resented the loss of freedom. The Taliban saw this resistance as a rejection of Islam itself. Their rule now degenerated into tyranny. People in the West, like many Muslims, were outraged by the Taliban attitude toward women, minorities, and the arts – as evinced by the destruction of the Buddhist statues.

By July 1998 the Taliban had already banned women from public places, jobs, and education. Next they banned television. In one simplistic sense, their action was understandable. It was through television that the threatening images came to Islam, and they had to be stopped. But their action was futile. There was no stopping the outside world and Islam had to come up with a better solution than simply banning it.

i Case Study Two: The Scholarship of Exclusion

To what extent were the Taliban's activities rooted in Islam? As an anthropologist I recognize much of Taliban political activity as coming from an understanding of traditional Pukhtun social behavior. In a patriarchal tribal society based on the notion of honor and modesty what the Taliban were doing made anthropological sense. But much of it was far from the spirit and learning of Islam.

Anthropologists confirm that there are many customs in Pukhtun society that are not Islamic. However they have been absorbed by the Pukhtuns, who identify so closely with Islam that they do not challenge them. Bride-wealth, or taking money for the bride, for instance, is un-Islamic and reduces the transaction to a sales bargain (see Ahmed 1980, 1991).

While Western commentators saw the Taliban as an "Islamic" body, few of them seemed to understand that, as much as Islamic fervor, the Taliban were driven by *Pukhtunwali* or the code of the Pukhtuns (see Ahmed 1980, 1991). Their treatment of women and minorities has more to do with *Pukhtunwali* than Islam. The laws of hospitality and revenge dominate *Pukhtunwali* (for tales of honor and revenge along the Pakistan–Afghan frontier, see Ahmad and Boase 2003).

Pukhtunwali explains why the Taliban would not surrender their guest bin Laden even though they faced death and destruction as a result. It also suggests that the laws of revenge will be activated and individuals or groups will extract vengeance for what they have suffered as a result of the war in 2001 and 2002. The Americans, the British, and their allies the Pakistanis would be the likely targets.

There are no limits of time or space in the implementation of *Pukhtunwali*. The saying about the Pukhtun who took revenge after a hundred years, remarking, "I took it quickly," is a well-known Pukhtun proverb (Ahmed 1975: 11). Nor in the taking of revenge do the Pukhtun care for those holding high office. It is well to remember that their victims have included a viceroy of India killed at the high noon of empire (Lord Mayo, killed in 1872) and a popular prime minister of Pakistan (Liaquat Ali Khan in 1951).

The tribal interpretation of Islam explains why there is sympathy for the Taliban in those parts of Muslim society where tribalism is strong, as in some parts of Saudi Arabia; it also explains the aversion to them where it is not, as in the middle-class sections of society in Cairo or Karachi influenced by the West. The Taliban also have some sympathy among Muslims who look for alternative answers to Western modernity.[2]

The Taliban are not only a political party; they are a social and religious movement, which spreads across Afghanistan and Pakistan and into parts of India and even Bangladesh. Although they are no longer in power in Afghanistan they still have large-scale support from those who think like them both in Afghanistan and Pakistan. People in the North-West Frontier Province in particular are notably sympathetic. It is well to recall that in the mid-1990s groups affiliated with the Taliban took over the Malakand Division. This was an unprecedented, full-fledged takeover of government.

The Taliban are not just knocking on the doors of Pakistan as many people believe; they are already inside. They may have few supporters in the urban areas or in the elite that rules from Islamabad but they have wide-spread support in the districts and rural areas. They also have sympathizers in the lower rungs of the army and bureaucracy. People see in them a group with more integrity and more commitment to Islamic values than their corrupt rulers who are often Westernised and thought to have "sold" the nation for personal gain. The elections of 2002 in which religious parties did dramatically well confirm their widespread support.

The educational roots of exclusion

To make matters worse, the social and political factors that explain the emergence of the *madrassah*s or religious schools, which produced the Taliban, remain largely unstudied. The emergence of the prototype *madrassah*s of Pakistan needs to be viewed in the context of the decline of Western-style education and administration and their loss of credibility for ordinary people. *Madrassah*s stand for a traditional system of education, which is the cheaper, more accessible, and more "Islamic" alternative to Western education.

The syllabus of a typical *madrassah* is exclusively Islamic in content. Its basis is the *Shari'a* (the Quran and the Sunna or life of the Prophet – together, the *Shari'a*). That is how it should be for an Islamic school. Islamic sayings exhort Muslims to acquire knowledge. One proverbial instance is "Seek knowledge, even unto China." China then, in the 7th century, symbolized the farthest non-Muslim civilization. It was a challenge to the imagination to even think of the journey.

Yet after numerous discussions in the 1980s and 1990s with teachers and an examination of *madrassah* syllabi I came to the conclusion that Muslim education faced a problem. It was too narrow and encouraged religious chauvinism. I noted that there are no non-Muslim philosophers or historians on those syllabi. Perhaps it is understandable why "godless" ones like Karl Marx would be ignored but what makes no sense is why others, like Max Weber, are left out. Worse, even Muslim ones, like Ibn Khaldun, who are thought to be too "scientific" and therefore not Islamic enough, are missing. The philosophy of the typical syllabus is reduced to what commentators call "political Islam" (Fuller 2003; Kepel 2002): Islam as a vehicle for all-encompassing change; Islam as a challenge not only to the corrupt local elite but also to the world order; Islam minus its sophisticated legacy of art, culture, mysticism, and philosophy.

After an initial period after independence when prestige was attached to Westernized schools, *madrassah*s began to flourish in the 1970s, most notably in South Asia; there are estimated to be 50,000 in Pakistan alone (Stern 2000). Remittances and grants from the Middle East provided funding and allowed central government channels to be bypassed. The war in Afghanistan against the Soviet occupation in the 1980s provided a global stage and a global cause to the youthful and zealous products of the *madrassah*s.

These *madrassah*s laid the foundations for the populist and militant Islamic leadership that would emerge in the 1990s. Mostly from poor, rural backgrounds, speaking only the local language, dressed traditionally, and with beards that asserted their Islamic identity, these students would become the warriors who formed the Taliban and go on to conquer Afghanistan. The word Taliban entered the global vocabulary.

The battle of Afghanistan against the Soviets was won not on the playing fields of the Muslim Etons but in the humble classrooms and courtyards of the *madrassah*s. Its outcome challenged and changed the already shaky educational and political structures in the entire region, not just in Afghanistan. The impact of the Taliban brand of thought, the frame of mind, the style of behavior and logic of argument, can be seen in different measure in Muslim groups from Los Angeles to Lahore.

The bitter anti-Western edge to the Taliban is recent. It comes from the Taliban believing that while their kin sacrificed their lives and land in fighting the Soviets as allies of the Americans, when it was over the Americans left them and their devastated land in the lurch. They will remind you that those now being called "crazies" and "extremists" by Westerners were once hailed as "freedom fighters" by the very same people. Their actions are partly motivated by a psychological compulsion to enrage and defy their critics.

Destruction, not defacement, was on the minds of the Taliban in 2001. Blowing up the Buddhist statues, particularly the towering Buddhas of the Bamyan valley in central Afghanistan, which had survived the ravages of past rulers, even Ghengis Khan, enraged people who cared for the cultural legacy of civilization. For Buddhists there was a religious dimension also. Although Buddha is not worshiped as a god he is the fountainhead of Buddhism. That is why, along with the Dalai Lama, some of the most important figures of the Buddhist world attempted to dissuade the Taliban from destroying the statues. The refusal of the Taliban once again created an unmitigated global PR disaster for Islam.

Taliban hero

Explaining the Taliban, Karen Armstrong, the noted writer on religions, gave the example of Akbar, the Mughal emperor, and argued that the Taliban were falling away from this model ("Breaking the Sacred," *New York Times*, March 11, 2001). She, unusually, missed the point. Unusually, because she understands so well how people are attempting to interpret faith in our world (see Armstrong 2000).

Akbar was never a model for the Taliban or their Afghan ancestors. Indeed Akbar and his Mughal family were always considered "the enemy." Babar, the founder of the Mughal dynasty in Delhi, came from Farghana, north of what is now Afghanistan, and was opposed by the Afghans. Akbar himself was far too influenced by Hinduism to ever be a legitimate model for the Afghans. The Afghans abhor his thousand wives and syncretized religion, the *Din-e-Ilahi*, which to them expressed a casual attitude to Islam.

Armstrong should have spotted the historical figure most relevant to the Taliban. This was Mahmud of Ghaznavi, one of the most important historical figures to emerge from Afghanistan, who, a thousand years ago, fell like a bolt of lightning on India. He raided Indian cities and plundered Indian temples. His famous – or notorious, depending on which historian is recounting the story – raid on Somnath inspired verses written by the renowned poet Allama Iqbal himself. When asked whether Mahmud would spare the huge idol at Somnath for gold and jewellery Mahmud is said to have replied: "I am an idol smasher not an idol seller."

I cited Mahmud of Ghaznavi as one of those key figures in South Asia who split the religious community down the center in my book *Jinnah, Pakistan and Islamic Identity: The Search for Saladin* (1997a). For most Muslims he is one of the greatest heroes of Islam, bringing their faith to the region and carrying it with the power of the sword. To most Hindus he is the symbol of Muslim oppression and fanaticism. There will be few neutral opinions on Mahmud. Even today both India and Pakistan have kept his memory alive to score their own points.

It was this line of thinking that Mullah Umar, the leader of the Taliban, referred to when he ordered the destruction of the statues and spurned the offer of the world to pay him if he spared them. The Afghans were looking back at a model in their own history to justify their actions today. They found one a thousand years ago. Smashing idols is thus a powerful symbol of faith for those who believe their monotheistic God is jealous of any images that distract from His worship.

Even today Muslims throughout South Asia – not only in Afghanistan – quote Iqbal's popular verse, proudly declaring that a true Muslim is an idol breaker not an idol seller. The Taliban therefore, far from falling away from Islamic models of tolerance as depicted by Akbar in India, were simply reaching back to a legitimate Afghan model of leadership.

The question is not the legitimacy of the model but why they were adhering to it. The answer is not so much that their aim was to antagonize the world – as they did so effectively – but that it was to make several gestures through this one big dramatic gesture. They at one and the same time asserted their sense of identity; they also expressed their disgust with the world that seemed to be indifferent to the suffering and starvation of their families, especially children and women, and more concerned with cultural artefacts; there was also the perverse glee of knowing that they could cause pain to a world that was so indifferent to their own pain. They told the world what they thought of it.

When the Taliban began to blow up the statues early in 2001 they took on more than they bargained for. Hindu extremists in India immediately threatened not only to blow up Muslim religious buildings in India but also to march on Mecca and Medina, the heart of Islam, and to destroy the ancient mosques and sites. Militants burned the Quran. The act enflamed Muslim public opinion as the Quran is considered the word of God. Once again Muslim behavior was drawing the world into a confrontation; once again it was Islam challenging the rest of the world.

The Americans may have hammered the Taliban in Afghanistan in 2001 and 2002, but the war did little to counter the influence of the Taliban's kind of thinking elsewhere in the Muslim world. On the contrary, the sympathy for Afghanistan helped to throw a blanket over their misdeeds throughout the Muslim world.

The Muslim responses to the tragic deaths of September 11 were also revealing. While many people expressed sorrow they also noted bitterly that it was time for Americans to experience the pain and suffering that Muslims – like the Palestinians and Kashmiris – live with normally. Implicit in their reaction was a sense of gloating at the pain of others. The war in Afghanistan and the expression of crude anger against Muslims in the United States and Britain did little to win hearts and minds on either side.

ii   Exclusivists in America: The Debate in Cleveland, Ohio

The debate about the nature and directions of Islam is taking place wherever Muslims live. I heard it in Cleveland, Ohio, where I had gone to deliver the annual lecture to the Ibn Sina Society in October 2001. We had discussed whether to cancel the Cleveland event in the uncertainty following September 11. Some tension had developed between Jews and Muslims. The imam of the central mosque had made some anti-Semitic remarks and was in the news. Then a young man had driven into the central mosque, destroying the entrance. We decided to go ahead with the event in the hope that it would promote dialogue.

The night before the event, my host, Dr Zia Khan, a prominent Pakistani physician, had invited about 60 professional Muslims – Arabs, Iranians, and South Asians – to his home. The discussion at the dining table made clear the differences between the exclusivists and the inclusivists.

When I stated that Islam had suffered a major setback after September 11 (for a grossly un-Islamic act of violence), that every Muslim was in the dock as a result, that there was turbulence in the Muslim world, and that the Islamic ideal had been thrown further off balance, I was challenged by some Arabs and Pakistanis. They called September 11 a glorious event for Islam. The taking of innocent lives was justified, they argued, as September 11 was the continuation of a full-scale Islamic war taking place against Israel, which is backed by the United States.

I heard a similar debate when the Muslim Council of Britain hosted a dinner for me in London in July 2002.

I argued that the Quran could not be interpreted in two ways. Either the taking of innocent lives was allowed or it was not allowed. Since the Quran categorically prohibited it, Muslims had to either accept this or not accept the Quranic injunctions about killing. It was like the prohibition on alcohol. It was categorically not allowed. A Muslim could not say, "I will take a sip from time to time under certain circumstances." Many saw my point but some Arabs continued to argue; however their support in the group diminished as the evening wore on. But the debate was illustrative of the thinking wherever Muslims lived. The Islamic ideal was fractured and needed to be rebuilt if Muslims were to move forward in any meaningful and coherent manner.

There were many eminent Muslims and non-Muslims present at the lecture in Cleveland. In particular I welcomed Martin Plax, the head of the American Jewish Committee. Set against the background of the tensions at the mosque, the event helped to encourage dialogue.

We have established through the case studies above that there is an ongoing, sometimes simmering, sometimes explosive, conflict of civilizations; but we have also illustrated that there is a serious and committed movement toward dialogue. Let us now explore possible solutions and the kind of questions that need to be raised for the future.

7

Toward a Global Paradigm

i The Challenge for Islam

What September 11 confirmed was the ability of a few determined individuals to pull their entire civilization, whether it agrees or not with their thinking or actions, into a confrontation with other civilizations. If a group of Hindus demolishes a mosque in Ayodhya or Muslims blow up Buddhist statues in Afghanistan, their religions are associated in the world media with these acts of extremism.

The ultimate nightmare scenario

Now imagine the nightmare terrorist scenario of the destruction of the central mosque in Jerusalem, the holy city for all three Abrahamic faiths and the one city where the three live side by side and which has the potential to create positive interfaith interaction. The mosque there is one of the oldest and holiest in Islam. The Prophet took his fabled night journey to heaven from there, an occasion that is celebrated annually with fervor. Or imagine the impact of the destruction of Mecca, as suggested by an American editor.

If some trained and determined individuals were to

blow up these places – as some have threatened to do for political and religious reasons – the action would have the potential to trigger immediate world conflict. Islam could be set on a collision course with Judaism and Christianity. The "war" may not have military battles, because governments do not respond in apocalyptic terms, but Muslims, wherever they live, might be determined to take revenge by acts of violence. And if that were the case, few Muslims – however keen on dialogue – would want to be involved in attempting to explain what happened. Emotions would be too powerful for rational thought. Dialogue and understanding would simply be ignored.

If we are to prevent the world from lurching toward one crisis after another, one flashpoint to another, then we all need to radically rethink the relationship between our religion and other religions; a radical reassessment of each other.

Unless there is commitment to dialogue and understanding there will be little progress. There will be no hope of reversing the processes that have created hyper-*asabiyya* and consequently a post-honor world. And understanding cannot come without an appreciation of the depth of feeling in the Muslim world about the absence of *adl*, justice, *ilm*, knowledge, and *ihsan*, compassion and balance. To help re-create the Islamic ideal is therefore an essential objective of all – Muslims and non-Muslims alike – who want global harmony and peace.

What needs to be done?

In the short term the prospects for a harmonious relationship between Islam and the West and other world civilizations look uncertain, even pessimistic. In the longer term a great deal will depend on whether those who encourage dialogue and understanding will succeed or not.

What needs to be done? And can it be done in a manner that can involve Muslims and non-Muslims in a common endeavor? Before anything else we need to understand what is going wrong: to face the fact of the collapse of *asabiyya*; from this understanding flows all else. The equation of honor with violence is one direct consequence of the collapse of *asabiyya*. The need is to reconstruct notions and practice of justice, compassion, balance, and knowledge. This will divert the exclusivists, bristling with the need to maintain honor, from confrontation to accommodation, from conflict to consensus.

What Muslims must do

What is the priority for the Muslim world in the coming time? And how can the West best help?

The first steps are to stop demonizing each other; for Muslims to stop seeing a global conspiracy all around them, they must improve their understanding of the West beyond the stereotype of the Great Satan who is eternally plotting to exterminate Islam all the while indulging in an orgy of sex and violence.

Muslims need to put themselves in the place of the non-Muslims who see them as a threatening and anarchic force; of Jews in Israel surrounded by what they see as millions of Arabs united in their aim of the destruction of their state; and of Hindus in India flanked by Pakistan and Bangladesh, and, just beyond, by Iran and the Middle East, Muslim societies that to them appear in the grip of Islamic fervor.

The Muslim world needs to institute and ensure the success of democracy. While the practice of democracy in the Muslim world has been disappointing and is synonymous with corruption and mismanagement, in the end there is no alternative. It is the only system that allows corrupt leaders to be removed with minimal friction. The world can help by ensuring that elections are fair and free and that resources are provided in the holding of elections and maintaining of institutions that safeguard democracy.

Muslims must be able to feel that they can participate in the process of governance. They must feel that they are able to elect their leaders and that if those leaders are not able to deliver, that they can throw them out as well. Too many Muslim leaders are kings and military dictators. Many of them ensure that their sons or relatives stay on to perpetuate their dynastic rule. Most Muslims feel truly disenfranchised.

With a working democracy Muslims will be able to ensure that the gaps that are widening between the rich and the poor will be bridged. The sight of palatial mansions guarded by security guards carrying automatic weapons and, nearby, the miserable squalor of the shantytowns teeming with poor children, is common in Muslim cities. The redistribution of wealth must remain a priority of any democratic government.

Another priority is education. Muslim societies need to have access to affordable, high-quality education so that they can be put on a par with other developed societies. Education must not be restricted to the small Westernized elite. The majority who benefit from the *madrassah*s must also learn sciences, technology, mass media, and information about the world and its diversity.

Muslim education needs to emphasize the tolerant and compassionate nature of Islam. Only then will the central features of Islam re-emerge. When *adl, ihsan,* and respect for *ilm* resurface, there will be tolerance for scholars and for minorities in society. Most important: women will be given their rightful place in society.

Muslims must rediscover the tolerance that once char-
acterized their societies. We need also to point out what
Muslims sometimes gloss over or refuse to acknowledge:
There are far too many complaints about human rights
violations, especially concerning non-Muslim minorities,
in Muslim countries. This is because there is too little of
the Islamic spirit of tolerance and compassion. Why are
Muslims ignoring the Quranic instructions to "forgive and
be indulgent" [to the people of the Book, Jews and
Christians] (Surahs 2 and 109)? Why are they forgetting
that God's greatest names are the Beneficent and the
Merciful?

Consider the kidnaping, hijacking, torture, and blowing
up of ordinary people in churches, buses, and bazaars:
Where are those young men – and now women – getting
their inspiration? Why have Muslims abandoned one of
the most powerful and endearing features of Islam? Why
is the resistance invariably expressed in violence (as in
Palestine, Iran, Afghanistan, Algeria, Pakistan, Egypt)?
Why are the gentle teachers and mystics of Islam not
heard?[1]

Muslim leaders also need to worry about the social and
demographic trends in their countries. Muslim population
growth rates are among the highest in the world, the
literacy rates are among the lowest, the figures for health
facilities are unsatisfactory, and the life expectancy below
average. The chasm between affluent corrupt elites and
the majority population is growing ominously wide. All
this when a large percentage of the population is young,
jobless, and restless for radical change. For many, an
aggressive Islam, which easily translates into violence, is
the natural way out.

Finally, Muslims face another, greater, challenge, an
internal one: They need to rebuild an idea of Islam,
which includes justice, integrity, tolerance, and the quest

for knowledge – the classic Islamic civilization – not just the insistence on the rituals; not just the five pillars of Islam but also the entire building. Reducing a sophisticated civilization to simple rituals encourages simple answers: reaching for guns and explosives, for instance. Today, piety and virtue are judged by political action – often equated to violence – not moral integrity or spirituality.

What the West needs to do

The West, because of its global power, needs to take the initiative. The problem is that Western powers who now interact with the Muslim world appear to have no long-term strategy. Without some long-term clarity and understanding, the relationship will be a difficult and unsatisfactory one. To make matters worse, the interests of the multinationals – like those dealing with oil – seem to drive policy. In large parts of the world – not only in the Muslim areas – it is commonly believed that the West is interested in military action in Afghanistan and Iraq because the former provides access to potentially oil-rich Central Asian states and the latter could provide further oil supplies. We saw above how Asian intellectuals are seeing the "war on terrorism" as really a war for profit – Al-fayda (Arundhati Roy in the *Guardian*, September 27, 2002).

The West needs to respond to the Muslim world firstly by listening to what Muslims are saying and secondly by trying to understand Islam. With some patience and understanding the general desire to assist the Muslim world will take shape. If the West is able to focus on democracy and education there will be clarity both of vision and of objectives. This will also ensure that Muslims do not feel that the West is out to subvert Islam.

Listening and understanding are crucial. Take the most commonly used words about Muslims such as "fundamentalist" and "*jihad.*" Because the world media equate the former with an extremist, fanatic terrorist who is (invariably) Muslim, we can only wonder how many media people pause to ask: Can we legitimately apply a term devised to describe something in one culture (a certain brand of Christian behavior and thought) to another distinct culture? As Muslims by definition believe in the Quran – however actively or not they may follow its instructions – they are technically all fundamentalists. So then, is every Muslim on earth today an extremist, a fanatic, and a terrorist? No. Obviously not.

Among Muslims and non-Muslims alike, how many know that the notion of the greater *jihad*, commonly misunderstood as an aggressive act of religious war in the West, and which derives from the word to strive, was explained by the Prophet as the attempt to control our own base instincts and work toward a better, more harmonious world? The lesser *jihad* is to battle physically for Islam; that too only as a defensive action against tyranny and injustice.

The West can put pressure on Muslim governments – and it interacts with most of them overtly or covertly – to get their act together, to ensure justice, and to provide clean administration. Western governments can help for instance in education programs. Take the example of Pakistan. After September 11, Pakistan was to receive more than a billion dollars in American aid. How much of it will disappear as commissions and bribes? How much of it is earmarked for education? Is the syllabus of the *madrassah*s being improved? How much investment is being made in the libraries and the teachers' training programs?

The West must send serious signals to the ordinary

Muslim people – via the media, through seminars, conferences, meetings – that it does not consider Islam to be the enemy, however much it may disagree with certain aspects of Muslim behavior. The West needs to understand Islamic expressions of revolt as movements against corruption and lack of justice, not as anti-Western.

By recognizing the argument in this book – that Muslim societies are in a state of turmoil as a consequence of the breakdown in social cohesion and the resulting sense of anomie – the West can help Muslims rebuild their sense of dignity and honor.

The West needs to discourage the knee-jerk "nuke 'em" response to Muslims and the labeling of any Muslim act as "fundamentalist." It must learn to curb and control its Islamophobic tendencies. The international media and Western governments need to be more sensitive to Muslim society. The West needs to treat Islam in its reporting with the dignity due to a world religion. The Western media's generalized and intense contempt of Islam provokes many Muslims into an anti-Western stance. It also makes the position of those who talk of dialogue and moderation more vulnerable.

The common problems in this shrinking world need to be identified: drug and alcohol abuse, divorce, teenage violence and crime, ethnic and racial prejudice, the problems of the aged and the poor; the challenge of the growing sense of anarchy and rampant materialism; the sexual debasement of women and children; the depletion of our natural resources and ecological concerns.[2] The pandemic of AIDS that is devastating individuals, families, and entire societies in Africa and appears to be spreading in India, Russia, and China almost unchecked needs to be vigorously challenged. On all these issues Islam takes a strong, enlightened position. This is the real Islamic *jihad* and, if it is properly harnessed and understood, it can provide fresh, sorely needed strength to these most crucial global issues.

Besides, we need to put in perspective the dominant ideas of materialism and consumerism. We need to be able to appreciate the special destiny of our human lives and not be in awe of the technological developments that are challenging our spiritual lives. Such marvellous developments need to be at our disposal; we must not be at their disposal.

When Muslims look at their society they see fundamental problems; when they look outside, they also see major problems. That is why they feel under siege. And they see these problems on the mainstream television news and on the front pages of the world's newspapers. Most of the news is violent and not good for Muslims. Either Muslims are being killed or are killing; innocent people are dying. There seems to be no easy solution. This is true of the news from the Middle East, from Kashmir, Chechnya, south Sudan, and the Balkans. That is, the news from three continents – Europe, Africa, and Asia – is bloody and centered on the problems facing Muslims and their relationship with others. Unless some resolution takes place in these areas the unending cycle of violence will continue. The world needs to focus on resolving these problems and not on responding to them with increasing force; it has been established in human history that violence simply creates more violence.

Ethnic and religious violence is the dark and ugly side of human nature. To contain it and to combat it we need to first understand it. To examine ethnic and religious violence is not to look at the aberrant or the marginal or the temporary – the specialist's area of interest; it is to come face to face with our age, our nature, and our aspirations. The violence brings us face to face with the human condition.

In ethnic and religious violence the human race faces a moral collapse that leads to the most diabolical acts of cruelty. Our world has the capacity and the resources to tackle other pressing problems that we face, such as hunger and disease. We should do no less in response to ethnic and religious violence. Clearly, the global community is at some kind of dramatic crossroads, a cusp, and a critical point in history.

ii Questions for our Time

With Ibn Khaldun's cycle broken down – with the interpenetration of global religious cultures, with the intrusive spread of the media with its alien images and ideas that reach even the most remote homes, with the scholars silenced, with the growing sense of despair at the poverty and inequality in many parts of the world that challenges the notion of a compassionate God who maintains a balance in human society based on justice and order – we need to develop a post-Khaldunian paradigm. A new theoretical and methodological framework to study global society in the 21st century needs to be developed, one which would incorporate the notion of social cohesion and the new diversity of global society and therefore recognize the need for Andalusian tolerance. We need to discover a new General Theory of social science.

The unexpected and unpredictable expressions of religious revivalism today would have surprised the philosophers and sociologists of the modern age. Certainly Nietzsche,[3] who declared God dead, and even Weber, who saw the Protestant ethic as laying the foundations for a stable, safe, capitalist, and bureaucratic world, would have been surprised. For the former, God was back and it seemed with a vengeance; for the latter, He was busy challenging and upsetting the very order that He was supposed to champion. Perhaps Marx would be the most surprised. Religion is no longer an "opiate" numbing people into docility; it is more like "speed."[4]

Studying the idea of the divine

Studying the main global religions in interplay, sometimes clashing, sometimes in alliance, can provide a clue.[5] All the religions are in need of understanding as they are usually viewed through the lens of stereotype and caricature; but perhaps none more so than Islam, which continues to get bad press and evoke hostility.

The thesis about the clash of civilizations, which remains influential in some circles, rests on the assumption that the wars of this century will be fought along religious lines. It is therefore logical and urgent to understand what factors are responsible for the emergence of religion and how religion will be playing a role in deciding political developments in this century. However, we need to penetrate beneath the sensationalist nature of these theories and discover alternative ways of understanding society. I do not suggest that we accept each other's or all religions uncritically but that we understand them in order to make sense of what is happening in global society.

Asking questions

In this connection, certain questions need to be asked.[6] These questions are an outcome of the discussion in the previous chapters. Different civilizations look differently at the idea of the divine. Muslims are often attacked in the media for what is called revivalism or the resurgence of Islam, but religious revivalism is taking place globally, in Judaism and Christianity, in Hindu and in Buddhist societies. The "rediscovery" of the divine is noted even in Western scientific and intellectual circles once dismissive of religion (see, for example, Glynn 1999). We need to know how the different world civilizations view themselves and each other; we need to know what they see as their vision of the coming time; we need to view their ideas of "the end of time"; we need to heed the mounting clamor of those who see the signs of the apocalyptic end of time and wish to accelerate the process.

This raises our first set of questions: Why is there a revival of religions and how are people negotiating the idea of God or the divine? Is the revival a consequence of the processes of and transformations resulting from globalization? Is the explanation to be found in the weakening of traditional structures – like the family, the tribe, and the nation state – as anomic individuals look to religion to provide certainty in an uncertain world, continuity in a changing one?

Is the revival an attempt to (re)create *asabiyya* in order to (re)build "human civilization?" But can we apply Khaldunian theories to non-Muslim civilizations? Or to industrialized ones? Indeed, can they be applied to Muslim societies when there are no significant cyclical – or even linear – movements of tribal or rural people taking place any more in the way Ibn Khaldun described them?

Asabiyya, which presupposes exclusivity, glorifies the group. But God while universal and generous in His attitude to mankind is nonetheless possessive about praise. God certainly does not approve of sharing praise with rivals called "tribe" or "nation." By conflating God and the group, leaders of the community employ an effective strategy: The honor of the group can now be defended in the name of God. As a consequence we see the emergence of a frenetic, distorted and dangerous form of *asabiyya* –

one I am calling hyper-*asabiyya*. Thus God's vision of justice and compassion are set aside for the group's need for honor and revenge. To unlock the conundrum of hyper-*asabiyya* anthropologists who study communities and how notions of honor affect behavior need to be in discussion with theologians whose business it is to attempt to understand God. One without the other would only comprehend part of the entire picture.

Our second set of questions has a global resonance after September 11: Why is the understanding of the divine distorted through the prism of violence? Why are people so responsive to ideas of upholding honor through a crusade or religious war? Why are innocent people being killed and women being raped in the name of the divine? No religion encourages violence of this kind, and yet we see it on our television sets and read about it in the news. Is it the failure of the humanistic interpretation of honor and the triumph of the violent interpretation? How do we halt or reverse the process?

What do the death and rape camps of Srebrenica evoke for Muslims? The burnt-out neighborhoods and the raped and murdered bodies of Muslims in Gujarat? The rubble that buried so many people in Jenin? And let us put the shoe on the other foot. How do non-Muslims respond to the Muslim hijackers killing thousands of innocent people on September 11? To Muslims killing innocent civilians, Jews in Israel, Christians in Pakistan, and Hindus in India? The answer is not an optimistic one. It reflects fury and anger, more talk of revenge and more violence. The new generations across the religious divides will be informed by these events and the names Srebrenica, Gujarat, Jenin, New York, and Washington will become potent symbols of injustice and religious violence. Notions of justice, compassion, and learning – the core features of faith – will be even more difficult to realize. There are global implications in this for what scholars call the clash of civilizations.

Third, we need to ask: What is to be done about it? How can we convince men that abusing and raping and killing are dishonorable acts, not honorable ones? How do we rediscover what is good and noble in human behavior? How to move out of a post-honor world and recreate a humanistic idea of honor?

The way forward

I believe one answer lies in the idea and practice of the dialogue of civilizations with a view to understanding others. That will be the first step toward re-creating honor and dignity based in compassion in a post-honor world. It will also act as a check to the manic and almost crazed expressions of hyper-*asabiyya* in our time. We need to build the idea of *asabiyya* or group loyalty that encompasses global society or all mankind, not just the tribe or the nation. Surely this is not such an unrealistic dream when we consider it was being practiced centuries ago by the mystic figures who joined the traditions of all the great faiths. The motto of the Sufis, *sulh-i-kul*, "peace with all," is worth recalling. Mawlana Jalal al-Din al-Rumi, whose work is so popular in America today, and Ibn Arabi, are two examples from different ends of the Muslim world. Their thought and verses explicitly reflect the essential unity of the divine vision in synagogue, church, and mosque. Rumi's example is ironic after the events of September 11: the idea of a Muslim poet popular in America, born seven centuries ago in Afghanistan, the nation that in the aftermath of the "war on terrorism" was being vilified for the Taliban and bin Laden, points to the paradoxes – and the hope – of our world.

We need to rediscover the deep wells of mystic thought that lie in each civilization. We need to rediscover and reemphasize the higher levels of spirituality, expressed through mysticism, which join all the great faiths – and significantly include the non-monotheistic ones like Hinduism. We need to make a conscious attempt to rediscover the essential spiritual unity in faith that transcends ideas of group honor and identity. This is possible. Let me cite some examples at different levels of dialogue.

I saw expressions of the human spirit and confirmation of its essential unity in the unlikely location of the crypt of Canterbury Cathedral, one of the oldest churches in European Christendom, in early October 2002. It was a musical evening that brought together a Japanese flute master, the choir of the cathedral, and Moroccan Sufi musicians accompanied by an African-American jazz pianist. To me the sight and sounds of the angelic choir singing "Jesus Walking on the Waters" and the Moroccans singing and dancing in honor of the Prophet of Islam summed up the possibilities of cultural harmony in the 21st century.

The musical evening was the climax of a two-day conference in Canterbury, "World Leaders of Faith and Development," convened by Dr George Carey, the then Archbishop of Canterbury, and James Wolfensohn, the president of the World Bank. Between them, the man of God and the man of development issues, they attracted some of the leading figures of the world. Their initial idea to examine the spiritual content of development issues remains a controversial one, both in the Church and among economists. But its power is undeniable and perhaps it will provide the way in the uncertain future.

It is difficult to reproduce here a list of people who attended because it is difficult to choose from the luminaries. Besides, the full titles are too long and my space limited. Let me give you an idea: there was Dr Meir Lau, the Chief Rabbi of Israel; His Eminence Cardinal Theodore McCarrick; Lord Moynihan, the former Conservative Foreign Affairs spokesman in the House of Lords; the Most Reverend Winston Njongonkulu Ndungane; the Rt Hon. Clare Short, Secretary of State for International Development; His Holiness Shri Swami Agnivesh from India; Reverend Canon Gideon Byamugisha; Mr José Maria Figures, former president of Costa Rica and managing director of the World Economic Forum; and His Beatitude Anastasios, Archbishop of Tirana and All Albania. Illustrating that these distinguished religious leaders were in touch with cultural trends and to enlist the support of like-minded people, Bono (Mr Paul Hewson), the lead singer of the band U2, was also invited. Bono's interest in poverty, debt, and AIDS has won him recognition; *Time* magazine in its March 4 issue had a lead article "Can Bono Save the World?"

International gatherings of this kind are usually stiff, as people bury ideas in platitudes. We all want peace; we all want harmony; we all live in hope. Sometimes meetings like this degenerate into vituperative exchanges. Atavistic prejudices break out.

This time something different happened. It is not easy to explain why. Perhaps it was the personal chemistry. Perhaps it was the Japanese flutist who began each morning with an inspiring and moving melody. Perhaps it was the inspired setting of Canterbury.

The participants not only expressed the urgency of focusing on the real issues facing global civilization – poverty, AIDS, civil conflict – but also the healthy need for self-criticism. "The world," Dr Carey said, "is in a terrible mess." The faith communities need to work together. Only with this vision can issues of development and poverty be effectively tackled. Bono created a powerful image of the sorry state of the world. "God is on His knees to us and imploring us to save humanity. We must respond urgently."

These courageous people were prepared to challenge the stereotypes in their own communities. Mr Wolfensohn, who is driving this vision in the World Bank, admitted that the efforts of his bureaucracy, numbering 10,000, were improving but were still "inadequate"; Dr Lau shared with us how he had visited Palestinian patients in hospitals, sometimes even before their own families; the Reverend Gideon disclosed that he had contracted AIDS and by publicizing it he hoped to highlight the problem that is devastating his continent, Africa, and now threatens India, Russia, and China; Swami Agnivesh condemned the actions of his coreligionists who had embarked on a killing spree of Muslims which he described in his book *Harvest of Hate* (2002); His Beatitude told me that his interest in Islam had led him to write a book on the religion which is used in his church. He pointed out that few people knew how much Muslims revered Jesus and Mary. Indeed, there are more references to Mary in the Quran than even in the Bible.

For me perhaps the most significant remarks came from the Archbishop of Canterbury himself. I had pointed out to him the hurt and anger in the Muslim world as a result of the recent remarks about the Prophet of Islam made by certain well-known religious figures in the United States. The Prophet, I had pointed out, was revered and loved by Muslims, even by those who were secular. These remarks were damaging Western interests in the bazaars in the Middle East and in the villages of South Asia. They were convincing people that indeed there was a "crusade" against Islam. Such abuse only encouraged the extremists in Muslim society. It added fuel to the flames flickering around the idea of the clash of civilizations.

The Archbishop responded with passion. He said he would like to go on record that these remarks are "outrageous." He said the Prophet of Islam was a great religious teacher and that he admired the Abrahamic spirituality of Islam. Indeed he appreciated the strong commitment of Muslims to their faith. Such remarks appalled him because they degraded Christianity itself. Christianity by definition is about compassion, generosity, and hope.

I was grateful for the courage and compassion of the Archbishop. His remarks will no doubt help heal the wound caused by the insensitive remarks. It was precisely this inclusivist spirit of compassion and understanding that gave me hope.

On the way to Heathrow Airport for my flight to Washington DC, I read the main stories in the British newspapers. Edwina Currie had just published a book revealing her affair with John Major, the former British prime minister. The news had even knocked Saddam Hussein and the talk of war against Iraq from the front pages. We were back to sex and scandal, the staple of the media. It appeared unreal to me. I was still hearing the sweet sounds from the Cathedral crypt and my heart was uplifted.

On another level my course at American University, "Religion and International Affairs," provides another example. I invited Rabbi Kenneth Cohen, a chaplain of the university, to speak to my class. He used the concept of "three sisters" in describing the three Abrahamic monotheistic faiths. Sometimes they quarrel, sometimes they are friends; but they belong to the same family. Joe Montville, the noted Christian scholar of religion and statecraft, concurred. Professor AbdulHamid Abu-Sulayman, the president of the International Institute of

Islamic Thought, and a well-known Saudi scholar, declared to my class: I am a Jew, I am a Christian, and I am a Muslim. Islam, he was pointing out, accepts the religious legacy of the great prophets of Judaism and Christianity. Professor Abdul Aziz Said, a venerable scholar of Islam, explained the universal mysteries of Islamic mysticism. This inclusivist approach created a common bond for discussion in my class that included Jewish, Christian, Muslim, and Hindu students. My students felt moved and inspired; so did I.

There have been signs of change in the Muslim community too. I saw this in the Islamic Society of North America's Annual Convention in August 2002 (this is the biggest Muslim society of North America). The convention was one of their biggest ever (35,000 people registered) and the first to be held in Washington DC. I had been asked to give the keynote address, to chair a panel, "Dialogue of Civilizations," and to host the showing of the Jinnah documentary at the first film festival organized by the society.

On the eve of the first anniversary of September 11, I urged the delegates to go to the synagogues, churches, and mosques on that day. To go in the spirit of reconciliation. To build bridges. I condemned in the harshest terms the treatment of women (citing the rape case described in chapter 2, section ii) and the bombing of churches and hospitals in Muslim countries. There was far too much talk of clash, revenge, and retribution I complained; the emphasis on compassion needs to be at the center of understanding between and within civilizations. I reminded the distinguished audience of the poor state of education in Muslim society and the irony that *ilm* or knowledge was the second most used word in the Quran after the name of God. I said that the four- and five-million-dollar Muslim houses I was invited to impressed me. I would be more impressed if they had some books in them. Knowledge is the path to spiritual unity.

This was an unusual message for the gathering. There is a tendency toward flag-waving and trumpet-blowing on such occasions. World conspiracies are blamed for the plight of the Muslims. I was therefore taken aback at the response. At the end of my talk people stood up and clapped in appreciation. "This was long overdue," some young people said to me later. The events of the previous September, I suspect, had something to do with the shift in attitudes.

The panel on "Dialogue" received a similar reaction. The distinguished speakers were: Shahid Husain, a former senior vice president of the World Bank, Dr Ayub Khan Ommaya, neurosurgeon, and Enver Masud, author. Saeed Khan, a scholarly and articulate lawyer, representing the young generation, also joined the panel.

The response gave me hope because we need to be thinking in terms of what Ibn Khaldun called "human civilization" or, to use the contemporary phrase, globally. We may not like words such as "postmodernism" and "globalization," but only with the compassionate understanding of other civilizations, through the development of the scholarship of inclusion, can we resolve some of the deleterious consequences of globalization, such as the increasing gap between the rich and the poor and the growing sense of despair, especially in the latter. The tragic confrontation among the great faiths taking place in the Balkans, the Middle East, and South Asia, the mindless cycle of violence, must be checked in this century through the dialogue of civilization. Long-term work needs to be started to build the confidence of communities. Serious and urgent rethinking is required by policy-planners and policy-makers in the corridors of power, not only in Washington, London, Moscow, and Paris but also in Cairo, Islamabad, Kabul, and Tehran.

In conclusion

I have pointed out the links between globalization, the disintegration of society and radicalization on the one hand, and sexual intimidation, an aggressive, excessive group loyalty and ideas of honor on the other. There is cause and effect here. We have noted that victims of religious or ethnic intolerance in one part of the world are themselves aggressors in other parts, through the acts of those who share their religion or ethnicity. Every group appears to be susceptible to the virus. Ethnic cleansing, I have suggested, ranges from the outright barbarity of death and rape camps to more subtle but also traumatic cultural, political, and economic pressures brought to bear on a minority.

I suggest a formula for the new millennium: If justice and compassion flourish – and are seen to flourish – in the Muslim world, if its rulers are people of integrity, and if Muslims are allowed to practice their faith with honor, then Islam will be a good neighbor to non-Muslims living outside its borders and provide a benevolent and com-passionate environment to those living inside them. It will continue to resist attempts to subvert its identity or dig-nity. Resistance can take the form of a Jinnah or a bin Laden.

The events of September 11 appeared to push the world toward the idea of the clash of civilizations, but they also conveyed the urgency of the call for dialogue. The creative participation in the dialogue of civilizations, to find an internal balance between the needs and traditions of local communities and a world increasingly dominated by international corporations and political concerns, the committed search for global solutions to the common global problems confronting human society, and the quest for a just, compassionate, and peaceful order will be the challenge human civilization faces in the 21st century. To meet the challenge is to fulfill God's vision; to embrace all humanity in doing so is to know God's compassion.

Notes

Introduction: God's Gamble

1   I am using *The Meaning of the Glorious Quran*, translated by Marmaduke Pickthall (1938).
2   The idea of the unity of God (*tawhid*) is central to Islam.
3   See Safi 2001 for a fuller discussion.
4   See Bullock 2002 for a fuller discussion.
5   Fukuyama was unrepentant about one idea he had explored earlier (1998): Islam as a form of modern fascism (see "Destructive Creation: Can any good come of Radical Islam?" by Francis Fukuyama and Nadar Samin in *Wall Street Journal*, September 12, 2002).
6   I had spent the last decade in active interfaith dialogue and I now saw my work in ruins: "I've spent my life trying to repair the image of Islam. Has it all been in vain?" in the *Independent*, September 20, 2001.
7   See Ahmed 1992a; Barthes 1989; Foucault 1984; Harvey 1989; Jencks 1986; Kroker and Cook 1988; Lash 1990; Lyotard 1984; Turner 1994. Some scholars are not even certain we have moved out of the phase of world history called modernity and use the phrase "high" or "late modernity" (Giddens 1991).
8   The death and rape camps of the Balkans in the early 1990s suggest a failure of compassion, imagination – and emotion. Some scholars believe, therefore, that we live in an age of "post-emotionalism" (Mestrovic 1996).

9 Fukuyama has developed the concept of posthuman to describe a world dominated by biotechnology (2002).
10 I first used the term "post-honor" in "World without Honor?" in *The World Today*, October 1998.
11 The idea is contained in the simplistic division of the world into *dar al-Islam* – the land of Islam – and *dar al-harb* – the land of war. The concept can be traced to the origins of Islam. After the Prophet's migration to Medina, the town was declared *dar al-Islam* while Mecca, from where he fled, remained *dar al-harb* (Zepp Jr. 1992: 30; see also Abu-Sulayman 1993a and Sachedina 2001).

Chapter 1   Islam Under Siege

1 Many other people like the neo-Marxist scholar Tariq Ali (2002) were seeing the mirror image. Ali is equally critical of both American and Islamic extremism or "fundamentalism." He sees fundamentalism in both the America of George Bush and the Islam of bin Laden. The illustrations on the front jacket of his book, Bush in a turban and Taliban-style beard, and on the back jacket, bin Laden in a Western suit striking a presidential pose behind a podium displaying the seal of the president of the United States, carry the main content of his argument. For him "Allah's revenge" and "God is on our side" are two sides of the same coin. The "neo-colonial" and "imperialist" America is hated not only in the Muslim world. He describes the joy in Central America, Brazil, and China on hearing the news of the events of September 11: "The subjects of *the* Empire had struck back" (ibid: 2).
2 Ibn Arabi's poetic and philosophic vision is contained in these lines from one of his poems (see Menocal 2000, 2002):

> My heart can take on
> Any Form:
> Gazelles in a meadow,
> A cloister for monks,

> For the idols, sacred ground,
> Kaaba for the circling pilgrim,
> The tables of the Torah,
> The scrolls of the Quran
>
> I profess the religion of love;
> Wherever its caravan turns
> Along the way, that is the belief,
> The faith I keep.

3 I have not selected these names because they are relatively popular in certain circles in the West. They are highly regarded mainstream Muslim figures and act as a standard and inspiration within Muslim society.

4 Those who have taken this line, both before and after September 2001, include: Armstrong 2000; Esposito 2002; Fuller 2003; Fuller and Lesser 1995; Nasr 2002; Rosen 2002 and Foreword to Ahmed 2002a.

5 Samuel Huntington's essay, "The Clash of Civilizations?" (1993), and later book (1996), have generated a global debate about a supposedly inherent conflict between Islam and the West. What is not well known is that both the term and the idea came from Bernard Lewis's essay "The Roots of Muslim Rage," written several years before Huntington's (in *Atlantic Monthly*, September 1990). In this essay Lewis also rehearses the arguments in his book, *What Went Wrong?* (2002). Directly or indirectly the ideas of Lewis and Huntington have influenced most international contemporary writing on Islam: Akbar 2002, Benjamin and Simon 2002; Corbin 2002; Hiro 2002; and Spencer 2002. However, Huntington and Lewis ignore the fact that there are some 25 million Muslims living in the West, that some Muslim nations are "pivotal" for United States foreign policy, that many Muslim leaders are strongly pro-West much to the disappointment of their own people, and above all there is the strong possibility of the dialogue of civilizations through the rediscovery of the Abrahamic tradition. I am pointing out the complexity of the relationship between Islam and the West and the need

to understand it through the filter of ideas of honor, justice, and dignity.

6   Many intellectuals from developing societies – not necessarily Muslims – were critical of the United States. For a devastating critique of the United States, what it stands for and its doomed role on the world stage, see "Not Again" by Arundhati Roy in the *Guardian*, September 27, 2002.

7   Interview with Al-Jazeera television (Qatar), broadcast October 7, 2001, and rebroadcast regularly on CNN in the United States.

8   Muslims in authority were also quick to learn the vocabulary of the new world order. Even teachers on campus freely used the word "terrorist" to put down their students. The vice chancellor of Karachi University, for example, called in paramilitary forces in an excessive use of force and dismissed the demands of his students by announcing that their activity ". . . amounts to terrorism" ("Troops break up demonstration at University of Karachi injuring dozens of protestors" by Martha Ann Overland in *The Chronicle of Higher Education*, September 9, 2002).

9   Some scholars see America as having the potential to create a genuinely harmonious multi-religious and multicultural society (see Eck 2001). As Muslims become more visible, incidents against the community appear to be on the rise. Anti-Muslim incidents rose by 15 percent in the year 2000–2001 according to a report, "Accommodating Diversity", issued by the Council for American–Islamic Relations (CAIR) in August 2001. Also see Findley 2001. "These incidents, many of which involved denial of religious accommodation in the workplace (48 percent) or schools (15 percent)," notes the CAIR report, "included thirty Muslim employees in Minnesota who walked off the job because they were denied the right to pray, a correctional officer in New York who was denied the right to wear a beard, a woman in Illinois who was fired for wearing a religiously-mandated head scarf, Muslim students in Virginia who were told they could no longer hold obligatory Friday prayers in school, and even a shotgun attack on a

mosque in Tennessee that left one worshiper wounded." More committed and vigorous work needs to be done in this area, especially after the backlash against Muslims as a result of the events of September 11; for examples of the backlash see "Healing the Nation: The Arab American Experience After September 11: A First Anniversary Report", Arab American Institute, Washington DC, 2002. For a passionate statement see *American Muslims* (Khan 2002).

Chapter 2   What is Going Wrong?

1 A historian like Lewis would ask: "What Went Wrong?" (2002); a social scientist would want to know "What Is Going Wrong?" If we do not know the disease we cannot apply a cure.

2 Richard Falk points out: "To a large extent, this human rights discourse is unavoidably perceived, with varying degrees of justification and opportunism, as tainted by false universalism and is an expression of Western hegemony, one feature of which has been, and continues to be, the suppression of civilisational identity and difference – particularly Islam, which has historically been perceived as a threat by the West" (2000: 150); see also Barber 1995; Esposito 1992, 2002; Fuller and Lesser 1995; Halliday 1996; Izetbegovic 1993.

3 President Muhammad Khatami of Iran, in his text to the United Nations General Assembly in New York on September 24, 1998, strongly and clearly advocated a "Dialogue of Civilisations" (Muhammad Khatami, "Dialogue of Civilisations"; see especially pp. 12 and 13). The two doves on the text of the statement symbolized its content. For a detailed discussion of the concept see Segesvary 2000; see also Picco 2001.

4 World figures like Pope John Paul II (1994), Dr George Carey, the former Archbishop of Canterbury, former President Nelson Mandela and Bishop Desmond Tutu of South

Africa, Jonathan Sacks, Chief Rabbi of the United Hebrew Congregation of the British Commonwealth (2002), Britain's Prince Charles (1993), and others have been involved in their own ways in this kind of dialogue for many years. The list includes Muslims like Hassan bin Talal (the former Crown Prince) of Jordan, the Aga Khan, and Dr Mahathir Mohamad, Prime Minister of Malaysia.

5   Dr George Carey, the former Archbishop of Canterbury, along with James Wolfensohn, the President of the World Bank, launched the World Faiths Development Dialogue in 1998. The events of September 11 confirmed their prophetic vision and reinvigorated their zeal. I was asked to join as Trustee late in 2001 and was honored to accept.

6   There is a flourishing literature on globalization and much of it is useful; for a standard definition and exploration see Kottak 2000. See also Ahmed 1993d, 2002a and b; Ahmed and Donnan 1994; Ahmed and Shore 1995; Bauman 1998; Beck 1992; Benthall 1993; Braibanti 1999; Falk 1999; Giddens 1990, 1991; Huntington 1993; Izetbegovic 1993; Khatami 1998, Mandaville 2001; Micklethwait and Wooldridge 2000; Mische and Merkling 2001; Moynihan 1993; Nash 1989; Robertson 1991, 1992; Thompson 1990; Turner 1994.

Lewis approaches the same subject from a historical perspective (1998); Friedman from that of a journalist (2000); Mittelman that of a political economist (2000); Ali from that of a neo-Marxist (2002); Giddens from that of a sociologist (2000); and Kottak that of an anthropologist (2000). For a more apocalyptic interpretation, see Halsell (1986, 1999); Kaldor (1999); and Kaplan (1997).

7   See Ahmed 1992a and others above.

8   Giddens argues modernity itself, the very engine driving globalization, is a "Western project" (1990: 174).

9   Friedman equates globalization to Americanization (2000: xix).

10 For definitions and dilemmas of tribal groups, see Ahmed 1980, 1991 and Ahmed and Hart 1984.

Chapter 3   Ibn Khaldun and Social Cohesion

1   I know of few international scholars who attract the range and quality of scholars from such different backgrounds as does Ibn Khaldun. Among them, to name a few, almost at random, are Gellner (1981), Rosen (1984), Lings (1995), Mahdi (1957), and Dhaouadi (1997).

2   I wish to acknowledge the American University in Washington DC for keeping the memory of Ibn Khaldun alive by naming a Chair after him. I held the Fellowship (Chair) named in honor of Allama Muhammad Iqbal at Cambridge University for five years. For me now to write as the Ibn Khaldun Chair at another Western university is a singular honor because I believe that though the two, Iqbal the poet-philosopher and Ibn Khaldun the sociologist, represent different zones, different disciplines, and different approaches, together they provide a rich mine for contemporary scholarship and an authentic basis for the dialogue of civilizations.

3   Ibn Khaldun was studying society in the western part of the Muslim world. But the Khaldunian cyclical pattern of rise and fall of dynasties held in Central and South Asia as well. Tribes from Central Asia invaded India and gave it seven dynasties that ruled from Delhi, each one in turn becoming effete over the generations and giving way to those with stronger *asabiyya* from the north.

4   See *Human Development Report* 1995. Also see Burki 2001. Burki makes the telling point through a comparison of Pakistan, one of the largest Muslim nations, with a population of 145 million, and the United States: Pakistan has 72 million people under the age of 19, America 70 million, although the population of Pakistan is half that of the United States.

5   The figures compiled by international organizations which indicate the health of a society confirm this gloomy picture. Statistics for economic and social development in the Muslim world – if we broadly identify it as the area from Morocco to Indonesia – are generally unimpressive and poor in com-

parison to other regions (*Human Development Report* 1995;
also see *Arab Human Development Report* 2002).

6 Despite his debunking, the symbolic value of Gandhi is still
strong. Swami Agnivesh, one of Gandhi's supporters (Agnivesh and Thampu 2002), quoted the following contemporary popular Indian slogan to me: "Oh Gandhi! We are
ashamed your assassins are alive and well."

7 This *hadith* is found, for example, in *Sahih al-Bukhari*,
number 6763, and *Sunan Darami*, number 242.

8 Abdus Salam was hounded out of Pakistan as he belonged
to the Ahmadi sect that most Muslims in Pakistan do not
consider Islamic; see my article on the subject, "Pakistan's
Blasphemy Law: Words Fail Me," *Washington Post*, May
19, 2002.

Chapter 4   The Failure of Muslim Leadership

1 Some neo-Marxists still yearn for the old days of the Cold
War. Tariq Ali would like the Muslim world to heed the
message of his father an "orthodox communist" (2002: 17).
The last words of Ali's book want the Muslim world to
abandon Islam and "to lay the foundations of a truly
progressive, a socialist Middle East." Ali is forgetting the
Muslim experience with socialist leaders in the Middle
East: Assad of Syria and Saddam of Iraq. Socialism means
the secret police, assassinations, entire populations brutally
killed, and a society living in fear. The rise of Islamic
extremism in the Middle East is a consequence of the
failure of nationalist and socialist movements.

Chapter 5   Searching for a Muslim
Ideal: Inclusion

1 I discovered on arrival in Cambridge that the Iqbal Chair
was designated as the Iqbal Fellowship because Pakistan
had failed to provide the full committed funding.

2 *Living Islam,* broadcast in 1993, was based on my book *Discovering Islam* (2002a – originally published 1988). It has been shown thrice on TV in the UK, the last time in August 2001 as part of the BBC's "Islam Week," and in many other countries of the world. My accompanying book, *Living Islam: From Samarkand to Stornoway,* was translated into many languages (Ahmed 1993a).

3 See the documentary *Dare to Dream,* Montage Productions, UK, on the making of the *Jinnah* film.

4 See "Jews and Jinnah," *Friday Times,* March 28–April 3, 1977 and "Iranian Counsel on 'Jinnah,'" *Friday Times,* Lahore, Pakistan, May 16–22, 1997. Also see the documentary *Dare to Dream.*

5 See "Profile: Ambassador of Dialogue" by Shagufta Yaqub, *Pakistan Link,* July 13, 2001; courtesy of *QNews,* London, July, 2001.

6 The slander and innuendos were baseless and deliberately created as a crude strategy to divert attention from the gross irregularities exposed by the company, a fact which is confirmed by the audit report of Petra conducted in December 1997 by a British firm, Brown Mcleod and Berrie, Chartered Accountants, Cambridge. (Also see "The Jinnah film and Quaid Project Report from 7 March 1994 to 31 March 2000," dated June 9, 2000). The campaign succeeded in damaging prospects for the film. For an account, which exposes the well-laid plan behind the campaign, written on behalf of the company, see "Quaid Project Limited Letter to General Pervez Musharraf," Free Press Network, *Information Times,* November 14, 2002.

7 See some of the stories about this minister on Information-times.com: "The Venal Game of a Pakistani Minister" by Amir Mateen, August 4, 2002 and "Supreme Court Judge must investigate Nasim Ashraf" by Syed Adeeb, Chief Editor, *Information Times,* Special Report, September 23, 2002.

8 See "Pakistan's Treatment of Intellectuals" by Dr Masood Haider, *Pakistan Link,* January 25, 2002.

9 Prince Charles saw *Living Islam* and the accompanying

book (Ahmed 1993a) when I presented them to him in 1993, and he used them for his celebrated lecture on Islam and the West at Oxford later in the year ("Islam and the West," speech by the Prince of Wales, Oxford Centre for Islamic Studies, October 27, 1993).

10   Many British journalists gave me the title "Ambassador for Islam" (Hawkey 1995). See also editorial on the Jinnah Quartet: "Akbar Ahmed's Achievements" (*The News*, London, November 30, 1998).

11   The general release of *Jinnah* in Urdu and English in Pakistan in June was selected as the main event of the month in the annual review of the premier English newspaper of Pakistan, *Dawn* (December 27, 2000). The *Dawn* report concluded: "That the film is still highly viewable and outright uplifting is a testimony to the will power of the man behind it, Akbar S. Ahmed."

12   Professor Khurshid Ahmad, a leading scholar of the Muslim world and senior figure of the Jamaat-i Islami, called me the "Ambassador of Islam" in *The News*, London, June 2, 2000.

Chapter 6   Searching for a Muslim Ideal: Exclusion

1   For a case study illustrating the complex interplay of Pukhtun tribalism, Islamic leadership, and political opportunism of the state, see my *Resistance and Control in Pakistan* (1991); for a scholarly yet affectionate account, see Edwards 1996; for an objective yet sympathetic account by a native of Peshawar who knows the region and the people, see Hussain 2001; for a scintillating and incisive account of the Taliban in the context of their history and region by a British journalist, see Lamb 2002.

2   I encountered the influence of Taliban thinking at first hand when I was invited to deliver a keynote address to a major Muslim conference in Chicago in July 2001. The

chairman of the organizing committee informed me that when my name had been announced some people objected. We respect his scholarship, they said, but object to his promotion of the Jinnah model of leadership over that of bin Laden. I felt that they were failing to appreciate their situation as Americans and as good Muslims who must live with other civilizations in the 21st century.

Chapter 7   Toward a Global Paradigm

1   I will illustrate my point with the following example: Sheikh Nazim Adil al-Haqqani Naqshbandi, the archetypical Sufi master – wise and old and frail but with a smile on his face and love in his heart – came to Cambridge on March 8, 1996. He had many admirers especially among the British converts. But tense young Muslims had already prepared a welcome of protest. They removed the posters announcing the visit every time they were put up and then boycotted the meeting; for them Sufism was a dangerous heresy. But the event organizers worked hard to ensure the meeting was a success. I helped behind the scenes. The sheikh seated me on his right on the dais as a mark of respect and we compensated for the rude behavior of the young Muslims with the warmth of our welcome.

2   For an articulate and scholarly book on just how serious the destruction of the planet is, see Pimm (2001).

3   When Nietzsche declared God was dead, dubbed himself the Anti-Christ, and preached the nobility of barbarism and cruelty he underestimated the power of ideas to direct political events: The Nazis were inspired by this poisonous philosophy (Nietzsche 1966 and 1972). Nietzsche's philosophic successor Martin Heidegger continued the tradition, becoming and remaining an enthusiastic Nazi to the end.

4   Even Marxists recognize the resurgence of religion, calling it "fundamentalism" (see Ali 2002).

5   As an indication of the interest in religion even before September 2001, several of the most popular journals like

Newsweek, *Time*, and *US News and World Report* featured cover stories on religion (see their April issues). There has also been an outpouring of high-standard books on religion: for examples, Armstrong 2000, Eck 2001, Forbes and Mahan 2001, Johnston and Sampson 1994, Mische and Merkling 2001, Smith 2001, and Wuthnow 2001.

6 I intend to explore some of the questions raised in this chapter in the book I am working on – *Negotiating God: Global Society and the Idea of the Divine in the 21st Century*.

References

Abdelkader, Deina (2000) *Social Justice in Islam*, International Institute of Islamic Thought, Herndon, Virginia.

AbuSulayman, AbdulHamid (1993a) *Towards an Islamic Theory of International Relations: New Directions for Methodology and Thought*, International Institute of Islamic Thought, Herndon, Virginia.

AbuSulayman, AbdulHamid (1993b) *Crisis in the Muslim Mind*, International Institute of Islamic Thought, Herndon, Virginia.

Agnivesh, Swami and Thampu, Valson (2002) *Harvest of Hate: Gujarat Under Siege*, Rupa Co, New Delhi.

Ahmad, Aisha and Boase, Roger (2003) *Pashtun Tales from the Pakistan–Afghan Frontier*, Saqi Books, London.

Ahmed, Akbar S. (1975) *Mataloona: Pukhto Proverbs*, Oxford University Press, Karachi.

Ahmed, Akbar S. (1976) *Millennium and Charisma among Pathans: A Critical Essay in Social Anthropology*, Routledge and Kegan Paul, London.

Ahmed, Akbar S. (1980) *Pukhtun Economy and Society: Traditional Structure and Economic Development in a Tribal Society*, Routledge and Kegan Paul, London.

Ahmed, Akbar. S. (1991) *Resistance and Control in Pakistan*, Routledge, London.

Ahmed, Akbar S. (1992a) *Postmodernism and Islam: Predicament and Promise*, Routledge, London.

Ahmed, Akbar S. (1992b) "Bombay Films: The Cinema as

Metaphor for Indian Society and Politics" in *Modern Asian Studies*, 26, 2, pp. 289–320.

Ahmed, Akbar S. (1993a) *Living Islam: From Samarkand to Stornoway*, BBC Books, London.

Ahmed, Akbar S. (1993b) "New Metaphor in the 'New World Order'" in *Impact International*, March 12 – April 8, pp. 24–7.

Ahmed, Akbar S. (1993c) "Points of Entry: The Taj Mahal" in *History Today*, vol. 43, May.

Ahmed, Akbar S. (1993d) "Media Mongols at the Gates of Baghdad" in *New Perspectives Quarterly*, vol. 10, summer.

Ahmed, Akbar S. (1996) "An Islamic University on the Internet" in the *Independent*, July 20.

Ahmed, Akbar S. (1997a) *Jinnah, Pakistan and Islamic Identity: The Search for Saladin*, Routledge, London.

Ahmed, Akbar S. (1997b) *The Quaid: Jinnah and the Story of Pakistan*, Oxford University Press, Karachi.

Ahmed, Akbar S. (1998) "World without Honour?" in *The World Today*, Royal Institute of International Affairs, London, October.

Ahmed, Akbar S. (2001) "Ibn Khaldun's Understanding of Civilizations and the Dilemmas of Islam and the West Today" in *Middle East Journal*, vol. 56, no. 1, winter.

Ahmed, Akbar S. (2002a) *Discovering Islam: Making Sense of Muslim History and Society*, Routledge, London. [originally published 1988; new Introduction and Foreword by Lawrence Rosen]

Ahmed, Akbar S. (2002b) *Islam Today: A Short Introduction to the Muslim World*, I. B. Tauris, London. [originally published 1999; revised 2002]

Ahmed, Akbar S. and Donnan, Hastings (eds) (1994), *Islam, Globalisation and Postmodernity*, Routledge, London.

Ahmed, Akbar S. and Hart, David (eds) (1984) *Islam in Tribal Societies: From the Atlas to the Indus*, Routledge, London.

Ahmed, Akbar S. and Rosen, Lawrence (2001) "Islam, Academe, and Freedom of the Mind" in *Chronicle of Higher Education*, November 2.

Ahmed, Akbar S. and Shore, Cris (eds) (1995), *The Future of*

Anthropology: Its Relevance to the Contemporary World, Athlone, London.

Akbar, M. J. (2002) *The Shade of Swords: Jihad and the Conflict between Islam and Christianity*, Routledge, London.

Ali, Tariq (2002) *The Clash of Fundamentalisms: Crusades, Jihads and Modernity*, Verso, London and New York.

Arab Human Development Report (2002) United Nations Development Program Arab Fund on Economic and Social Development, United Nations Publications, New York.

Armesto, Felipe Fernandez (1995) *Millennium: A History of the Last Thousand Years*, Scribner, New York.

Armstrong, Karen (2000) *The Battle for God: Fundamentalism in Judaism, Christianity and Islam*, HarperCollins, London.

Banaji, J. (1970) "Crisis of British Anthropology" in *New Left Review*, no. 64, pp. 71–85.

Barber, Benjamin R. (1995) *Jihad vs. McWorld*, Times Books, New York.

Barthes, Roland (1989) *Barthes: Selected Writings*, edited and introduced by Susan Sontag, Fontana Press, London.

Baudrillard, Jean (1994) *The Illusion of the End*, Polity Press, Cambridge.

Bauman, Zygmunt (1998) *Globalization: The Human Consequences*, Polity Press, Cambridge.

Beck, Ulrich (1992) *Risk Society: Towards a New Modernity*, translated by Mark Ritter, Sage Publications, London. [originally published 1986]

Benjamin, Daniel K. and Simon, Steven A. (2002) *The Age of Sacred Terror: Radical Islam's War against America*, Random House, New York.

Benthall, Jonathan (1993) *Disasters, Relief and the Media*, I. B. Tauris, London.

Braibanti, Ralph (1999) "Islam and the West: Common Cause or Clash?", Occasional Paper Series, Center for Muslim-Christian Understanding, Georgetown University, Washington DC.

Bullock, Katherine (2002) *Rethinking Muslim Women and the Veil: Challenging Historical and Modern Stereotypes*, International Institute of Islamic Thought, Herndon, Virginia.

Burki, Shahid Javed (2001) "Population as an Asset" in *Pakistan Link*, August 10.

Catherwood, Christopher (2002) *Why the Nations Rage: Killing in the Name of God*, Rowman & Littlefield, Lanham, Maryland.

Charles, Prince of Wales (1993) "Islam and the West," speech at Oxford Centre for Islamic Studies, Oxford, October 27.

Chase, Robert et al. (1996) "Pivotal States and US Strategy" in *Foreign Affairs*, January/February, vol. 74, issue 1.

Chaucer, Geoffrey (1977) *The Canterbury Tales*, Penguin Books, London.

Cohen, Stephen P. (2001) *India: Emerging Power*, Brookings Institution Press, Washington DC.

Cole, David, Dempsey, James X. and Goldberg, Carole E. (eds) (2002) *Terrorism and the Constitution: Sacrificing Civil Liberties in the Name of National Security*, New Press, New York.

Collins, Larry and Lapierre, Dominique (1994) *Freedom at Midnight*, Vikas, New Delhi. [originally published 1976]

Connor, Walker (1993) "Beyond Reason: The Nature of the Ethnonational Bond," Annual ERS/LSE Lecture, 1992, in *Ethnic and Racial Studies*, vol. 16. no. 3, July.

Corbin, Jane (2002) *Al-Qaeda*, Nation/Thunder's Mouth, New York.

Dalrymple, William (1994) *City of Djinns: A Year in Delhi*, Flamingo: HarperCollins, London.

Daniel, Norman (1960) *Islam and the West: The Making of an Image*, Edinburgh University Press, Edinburgh.

Dennis, Lisl and Dennis, Landt (2001) *Living in Morocco: Design from Casablanca to Marrakesh*, Thames and Hudson, New York.

Dershowitz, Alan M. (2002) *Why Terrorism Works: Understanding the Threat, Responding to the Challenge*, Yale University Press, New Haven.

Dhaouadi, Mahmoud (1997) *New Explorations into the Making of Ibn Khaldun's Umran Mind*, A. S. Noordeen, Kuala Lumpur.

Duran, Khalid (2001) *Children of Abraham: An Introduction to*

Islam for Jews, American Jewish Committee, distributed by Ktav Publishing House, Hoboken, NJ.

Durkheim, Emile (1964) *The Division of Labour in Society*, Free Press, New York.

Durkheim, Emile (1966) *Suicide: A Study in Sociology*, Free Press, New York.

Eck, Diana L. (2001) *A New Religious America: How a "Christian Country" has become the World's Most Religiously Diverse Nation*, HarperSanFrancisco, a Division of HarperCollins, New York.

Edwards, David B. (1996) *Heroes of the Age: Moral Fault Lines on the Afghan Frontier*, University of California Press, Berkeley, CA.

Elst, Koenraad (1992) *Negationism in India: Concealing the Record of Islam*, Voice of India, New Delhi.

Esposito, John L. (1992) *The Islamic Threat: Myth or a Reality?* Oxford University Press, New York.

Esposito, John L. (2002) *Unholy War: Terror in the Name of Islam*, Oxford University Press, New York.

Falk, Richard (1999) *Predatory Globalization: A Critique*, Polity Press, Cambridge.

Falk, Richard (2000) *Human Rights Horizons: The Pursuit of Justice in a Globalizing World*, Routledge, New York and London.

al-Fattah, Anisa Abd (2002) "When Time Stood Still in Jenin" in *Middle East Affairs Journal*, vol. 8. no. 1–2, winter/spring.

Findley, Paul (2001) *Silent No More: Confronting America's False Images of Islam*, Amana Publications, Beltsville, Maryland.

Forbes, Bruce David and Mahan, Jeffrey H. (eds) (2001) *Religion and Popular Culture in America*, University of California Press, Berkeley, CA.

Foucault, Michel (1984) *The Foucault Reader*, edited by Paul Rabinow, Penguin Books, London.

Friedman, Thomas (2000) *The Lexus and the Olive Tree: Understanding Globalization*, Farrar, Straus and Giroux, New York.

Fukuyama, Francis (1998) *The End of History and the Last Man*, Bard, New York.

Fukuyama, Francis (2002) *Our Posthuman Future: Consequences of the Biotechnology Revolution*, Farrar, Straus and Giroux, New York.

Fuller, Graham E. (2003) *The Future of Political Islam*, Palgrave, St Martin's Press, New York.

Fuller, Graham E. and Lesser, Ian O. (1995) *A Sense of Siege*, Westview/RAND, Boulder, Colorado.

Gellner, Ernest (1981), *Muslim Society*, Cambridge University Press, Cambridge.

Gellner, Ernest (1983) *Nations and Nationalism*, Blackwell, Oxford.

Giddens, Anthony (1978) *Durkheim*, Fontana Modern Masters, London.

Giddens, Anthony (1990) *The Consequences of Modernity*, Polity Press, Cambridge.

Giddens, Anthony (1991) *Modernity and Self-Identity: Self and Society in the Late Modern Age*, Polity Press, Cambridge.

Giddens, Anthony (2000) *Runaway World: How Globalisation is Reshaping our Lives*, Routledge, London.

Glynn, Patrick (1999) *God: The Evidence – The Reconciliation of Faith and Reason in a Postsecular World*, Forum: Prima Publishing, Rocklin, CA.

Goldberg, Danny, Goldberg, Victor and Greenwald, Robert (eds) (2002) *It's a Free Country: Personal Freedom in America after September 11*, Akashic Books, Brooklyn, New York.

Goldberg, Jeffrey (2000) "The Education of a Holy Warrior" in *New York Times Magazine*, June 25.

Golwalkar, Madhav Sadashiv (1938) *We or Our Nationhood Defined*, Bharat Prakashan Press, Nagpur, India.

Golwalkar, Madhav Sadashiv (1966) *Bunch of Thoughts*, Kesari Press, Bangalore, India.

Goytisolo, Juan (1993) "Terror Town" in *New Statesman and Society*, December 17–31.

Haider, Masood (2002) "Pakistan's Treatment of Intellectuals" in *Pakistan Link*, January 25.

Halliday, Fred (1996) *Islam and the Myth of Confrontation*, I. B. Tauris, London.

Halsell, Grace (1986) *Prophecy and Politics: Militant Evangelists on the Road to Nuclear War*, Lawrence Hill and Co. Westport, Connecticut.

Halsell, Grace (1999) *Forcing God's Hand – Why Millions Pray for a Quick Rapture – and Destruction of Planet Earth*, Crossroads Int. Publishing, Washington DC.

Harvey, David (1989) *The Condition of Postmodernity: The Enquiry into the Origins of Cultural Change*, Blackwell, Oxford.

Hawkey, Ian (1995) "Ambassador for Islam" in *CAM: The University of Cambridge Alumni Magazine*, Easter Term.

Heston, W. L. and Nasir, Mumtaz (undated) *The Bazaar of the Story Tellers*, Lok Virsa Publishing House, Islamabad.

Hiro, Dilip (2002) *War without End*, Routledge, London.

Hodgson, M. G. S. (1974) *The Venture of Islam*, 3 vols, University of Chicago Press, Chicago.

Hourani, Albert (1991) *A History of the Arab Peoples*, Faber and Faber, London.

Hoyt, Michael (2000) *Captive in the Congo: A Consul's Return to the Heart of Darkness*, Naval Institute Press, Annapolis, Maryland.

Human Development Report (1995) United Nations Development Program, Oxford University Press, Oxford and New York.

Huntington, Samuel P. (1993) "The Clash of Civilizations?" in *Foreign Affairs*, summer, vol. 72, issue 3.

Huntington, Samuel P. (1996) *The Clash of Civilizations and the Remaking of World Order*, Simon and Schuster, New York.

Hussain, S. Amjad (2001) *The Taliban and Beyond: A Close Look at the Afghan Nightmare*, BWD Publishing, Perrysburg, Ohio.

Izetbegovic, Alija Ali (1993) *Islam between East and West*, American Trust Publications, Indianapolis.

Jencks, Charles (1986), *What is Post-Modernism?*, Academy, London.

Jeremias, Joachim (1964) *Unknown Sayings of Jesus*, SPCK, London.

John Paul II (1994) *Crossing the Threshold of Hope*, Alfred A. Knopf, New York.

Johnston, Douglas and Sampson, Cynthia (eds) (1994) *Religion*,

The Missing Dimension of Statecraft, Oxford University Press, Oxford and New York.

Kaldor, Mary (1999) *New and Old Wars: Organized Violence in a Global Era*, Polity Press, Cambridge.

Kaplan, Robert (1997) *The End of the Earth: From Togo to Turkmenistan, from Iran to Cambodia, a Journey to the Frontiers of Anarchy*, Vintage Books, New York.

Kepel, Gilles (2002) *Jihad: The Trail of Political Islam*, I. B. Tauris, London.

Khaldun, Ibn (1969) *The Muqaddimah: An Introduction to History*, translated by Franz Rosenthal, Princeton University Press, Princeton.

Khan, M. A. Muqtedar (2002) *American Muslims: Bridging Faith and Freedom*, Amana Publications, Beltsville, Maryland.

Khatami, Muhammad (1998) "Dialogue of Civilisations", speech to United Nations General Assembly, New York, September 24.

Kimball, Charles (2002) *When Religion Becomes Evil*, Harper-SanFrancisco, a Division of HarperCollins, New York.

Kipling, Rudyard (1960) *Kim*, Macmillan Press, London.

Kottak, Conrad Phillip (2000) *Cultural Anthropology*, McGraw-Hill, Higher Education, Boston, New York, London.

Kramer, Martin (2001) *Ivory Towers on Sand: The Failure of Middle Eastern Studies in America*, Washington Institute for Near East Policy, Washington DC.

Kroker, Arthur and Cook, David (1988) *The Postmodern Scene: Excremental Culture and Hyper-aesthetics*, Macmillan Education, London.

Lamb, Christina (2002) *The Sewing Circles of Herat: My Afghan Years*, HarperCollins, London and New York.

Lash, Scott (1990) *Sociology of Postmodernism*, Routledge, London.

Lebor, Adam (1997) *A Heart Turned East: Among the Muslims of Europe and America*, Little, Brown, London.

Lee, Christopher (1997) *Tall, Dark and Gruesome*, Midnight Marquee Press, London.

Lewis, Bernard (1998) *The Multiple Identities of the Middle East*, Schocken Books, New York.

Lewis, Bernard (2002) *What Went Wrong? Western Impact and Middle Eastern Response*, Oxford University Press, New York.

Lindholm, Charles (1982) *Generosity and Jealousy: The Swat Pukhtun of Northern Pakistan*, Columbia University Press, New York.

Lings, Martin (1995) *What is Sufism?* Islamic Texts Society, Cambridge.

Loizos, Peter (1981) *The Heart Grown Bitter: A Chronicle of Cypriot War Refugees*, Cambridge University Press, Cambridge.

Lyotard, Jean-François (1984) *The Post-Modern Condition: A Report on Knowledge*, translated by G. Bennington and B. Masumi, University of Minnesota Press, Minneapolis.

Mahdi, Muhsin (1957) *Ibn Khaldun's Philosophy of History: A Study in the Foundation of the Science of Culture*, University of Chicago Press, Chicago.

Mahdi, Muhsin (1968) "Ibn Khaldun" in *International Encyclopedia of the Social Sciences*, edited by David L. Sills, vol. 7, Macmillan, New York.

Makiya, Kanan (1993) *Cruelty and Silence: War, Tyranny, Uprising, and the Arab World*, Jonathan Cape, London.

Mandaville, Peter (2001) *Transnational Muslim Politics*, Routledge, London.

Masud, Enver (2002) *The War on Islam*, Madrasah Books, An Imprint of The Wisdom Fund, Washington DC.

Menocal, María Rosa (2000)"Culture in the Time of Tolerance: *Al-Andalus* as a Model of Our Own Time," Yale Law School Occasional Papers, second series, no. 6.

Menocal, María Rosa (2002) *Ornament of the World*, Little, Brown, New York.

Mestrovic, Stjepan G. (1994) *The Balkanisation of the West: The Confluence of Postmodernism with Postcommunism*, Routledge, London.

Mestrovic, Stjepan G. (ed.) (1996) *Genocide after Emotion: The Postemotional Balkan War*, Routledge, London and New York.

Micklethwait, John and Wooldridge, Adrian (2000) *A Future*

Perfect: The Challenge and Hidden Promise of Globalization, Times Books, New York.

Mische, M. Patricia and Merkling, Melissa (2001) *Towards a Global Civilisation? The Contribution of Religions*, Peter Lang, New York.

Mittelman, James (2000) *The Globalization Syndrome: Transformation and Resistance*, Princeton University Press, Princeton.

Mohamad, Mahathir (2001) *Islam and the Muslim Ummah*, Prime Minister's Office, Putrajaya, Malaysia.

Moynihan, Daniel Patrick (1993) *Pandaemonium: Ethnicity in International Politics*, Oxford University Press, Oxford.

Najjar, Abdal Majid al (2000) *The Viceregency of Man: Between Revelation and Reason*, International Institute of Islamic Thought, Herndon, Virginia.

Nash, Manning (1989) *The Cauldron of Ethnicity in the Modern World*, University of Chicago Press, Chicago.

Nasr, Seyyed Hossein (2002) *The Heart of Islam: Enduring Values of Humanity*, HarperSanFrancisco, a Division of Harper-Collins, New York.

Nehru, Jawaharlal (1941) *Towards Freedom: An Autobiography*, John Day, New York. [originally published 1936]

Nietzsche, Friedrich (1966) *Beyond Good and Evil*, translated by Walter Kaufmann, Vintage, New York.

Nietzsche, Friedrich (1972) *Twilight of the Idols: The Anti-Christ*, translated by R. J. Hollingdale, Penguin, Harmondsworth, Middlesex.

Oak, P. N. (1990) *Some Blunders of Indian Historical Research*, Bharati Sahitya Sadan, New Delhi.

Padgaonkar, Dileep (ed.) (1993) *When Bombay Burned*, UBS Publishers and Distributors, New Delhi.

Pearson, Robert P. and Clark, Leon E. (2002) *Through Middle Eastern Eyes*, Apex Press, New York.

Picco, Giandomenico. (2001) "A Dialogue Among Civilisations" in *Seton Hall Journal of Diplomacy and International Relations*, vol. 2, no. 1, winter/spring, pp. 5–10.

Pimm, Stuart L. (2001) *The World According to Pimm: A Scientist Audits the Earth*, McGraw-Hill, New York.

Poggi, Gianfranco (2000) *Durkheim*, Oxford University Press, New York and Oxford.

Quran (1938) *The Meaning of the Glorious Quran*, translated by Marmaduke Pickthall, Government Central Press, Hyderabad-Deccan, India.

Qutb, Sayyid (n.d.) *Milestones*, Iowa University Publishing Co., Cedar Rapids.

Rashid, Ahmed (2000) *Taliban: Militant Islam, Oil and Fundamentalism in Central Asia*, Yale University Press, New Haven and London.

Reston, James, Jr (2002) *Warriors of God: Richard the Lionheart and Saladin in the Third Crusade*, Anchor Books, New York.

Robertson, Roland (1991) "The Globalisation Paradigm: Thinking Globally" in D. G. Bromley (ed.) *Religion and Social Order*, JAI Press, Greenwich, Connecticut, pp. 207–24.

Robertson, Roland (1992) *Globalisation: Social Theory and Global Culture*, Sage Publications, London.

Rosen, Lawrence (1984) *Bargaining for Reality: The Construction of Social Relations in a Muslim Community*, University of Chicago Press, Chicago.

Rosen, Lawrence (2002) *The Culture of Islam: Changing Aspects of Contemporary Muslim Life*, University of Chicago, Chicago and London.

Sachedina, Abdulaziz (2001) *The Islamic Roots of Democratic Pluralism*, Oxford University Press, Oxford.

Sacks, Jonathan (2002) "The Dignity of Difference: Avoiding the Clash of Civilisations," Foreign Policy Research Institute WIRE www.fpri.org, vol. 10, no. 3, July.

Safi, Louay M. (2001) *Peace and the Limits of War: Transcending Classical Conception of Jihad*, International Institute of Islamic Thought, Herndon, Virginia.

Said, Edward W. (1978) *Orientalism*, Penguin Books, New York.

Said, Edward (1993) *Culture and Imperialism*, Chatto and Windus, London.

Segesvary, Victor (2000) *Dialogue of Civilisations: An Introduction to Civilisational Analysis*, United Press of America, Lanham, Maryland.

Shah, Idries (1990) *The Sufis*, Doubleday, New York.

Sherif, M. A. (1994) *Searching for Solace: A Biography of Abdullah Yusuf Ali, Interpreter of the Qur'an*, Islamic Book Trust, Kuala Lumpur, Malaysia.

Smith, Huston (2001) *Why Religion Matters: The Fate of the Human Spirit in an Age of Disbelief*, HarperSanFrancisco, a Division of HarperCollins, New York.

Spain, J. W. (1963) *The Pathan Borderland*, Mouton, The Hague.

Spencer, Robert (2002) *Islam Unveiled: Disturbing Questions about the World's Fastest-Growing Faith*, Encounter, San Francisco.

Stern, Jessica (2000) "Pakistan's Jihad Culture" in *Foreign Affairs*, November/December, vol. 79, issue 6.

Thompson, John B. (1990) *Ideology and Modern Culture*, Polity Press, Cambridge.

Turner, Bryan S. (1994) *Orientalism, Postmodernism and Globalism: Intellectuals in the Modern World*, Routledge, London.

Varshney, Ashutosh (2002) *Ethnic Conflict and Civic Life: Hindus and Muslims in India*, Yale University Press, New Haven and London.

Vollmann, William T. (2000) "Across the Divide: What do the Afghan People Think of the Taliban?" in *New Yorker*, May 15.

Worsley, P. M. (1966) "The End of Anthropology?", paper for 6th World Congress of Sociology, mimeo.

Wuthnow, Robert (2001) *After Heaven: Spirituality in America since the 1950s*, University of California Press, Berkeley.

Yaqub, Shagufta (2001) "Profile: Ambassador of Dialogue" in *QNews*, July; reprinted *Pakistan Link*, July 13.

Yusuf, Feyyaz (1993) "Christian Radicalism Stirs the Serbs" in *QNews*, December 10–17, London.

Zepp Jr, Ira G. (1992) *A Muslim Primer: Beginner's Guide to Islam*, Wakefield Editions, Westminster, Maryland.

Index

Note: Where the endnotes for more than one chapter appear on a single page, notes of the same number are differentiated by the addition of a letter, e.g. 180 n.1a.

INDEX OF QURANIC REFERENCES